For all who are unwilling to settle for a life that is anything less than the life they are capable of living.

Passionate Living

Through

Passive Investing

By

George Roberts III, Ph.D.

Table of Contents

Dedication

To my wonderful wife, Mary, for being understanding about the time spent dedicated to this work. And to my two sons, may you enjoy all the extraordinary opportunities that this amazing land has to offer. Also, to my readers, may this book inspire and propel you on the next leg of your wealth and wellness journey. May you live a life of creativity and adventure, a life that reflects your truest self. To Amanda Accica of Argentine Tango Detroit; your confidence in me has meant the world to me. You and Donato Juarez are the best teachers anyone could ever hope for. Finally, to all who know that greatness is achievable and who strive daily to push back the frontiers of what is possible in their own lives.

Acknowledgments

Thank you https://www.qrcode-monkey.com/ for the free for commercial use QR codes. Also, thank you to my favorite Fiverr.com freelancer and financial author, Kristin K (@Cr8mom). Finally, a BIG thank you to my friends and colleagues who provided editorial suggestions Jerome Lewis, Shawn Griffith, and Peter Turner. You are my encouragement, my advisors, my support, and most importantly of all, my friends.

Disclaimer

This book is provided for informational purposes only and is not intended to provide legal, tax, or other professional advice, nor should it be relied upon as such. The author assumes no responsibility for any actions taken or not taken by the reader. Do your own due diligence and be sure to consult legal, tax as well as other professionals as appropriate. Use of this book constitutes acceptance of this disclaimer. Happy investing!

Join the **Passionate Living Through Passive Investing** Facebook Community!

Make this book come alive by sharing your personal story of investing and adventurous living with this vibrant tribe of extraordinary people. Your story will inspire others to make their lives more successful and passionate. Join our free Facebook community by scanning the QR code below. **#PassionateInvesting**

Introduction

"The Journey of a thousand miles begins with a single step."

-Lao Tzu

I am predicting that this isn't the first book on finance and passive investing you have picked up, am I right? Call me crazy, but as an award-winning data scientist, I made predictions for a living. Most books on passive income preach about achieving financial freedom through rigid formulas—build enough passive income to cover your bills, retire early, and, only then, fully live the dream. While effective, the traditional approach puts your quality of life while you build your financial empire on the back burner. Rather than regurgitating this familiar advice, let's embark on a revolutionary journey together.

Instead of focusing on the "freedom number"—the passive income needed to cover expenses and retire, I will focus here instead on maximizing your 'freedom quotient' - the percentage of time you spend on activities that ignite your passion. By nurturing this passion, we create a virtuous cycle whereby increased passive income fuels greater fulfillment, naturally leading to financial independence over time. We're about to unveil a novel approach prioritizing passion and fulfillment from the outset, guiding you to grow your passive income alongside a more prosperous, more fulfilling life.

Unlike the elusive "freedom number," which can fluctuate as the price tag on your life and dreams change, your "freedom quotient" remains constant. It's about finding enduring happiness in a life aligned with your truest core values—a life we'll build together, step by step.

Are you ready to explore your freedom quotient? Begin by taking this self-assessment to gauge where you are now to help you chart your path forward.

How much passion do you feel in your professional life?

Passion Meter

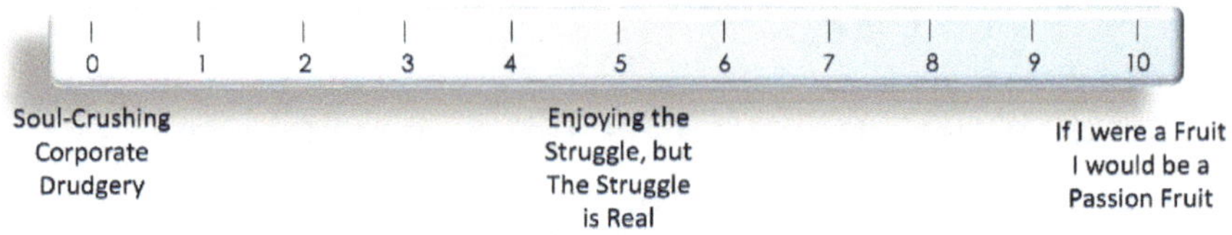

What percentage of your time is spent doing things you enjoy?

Freedom Quotient

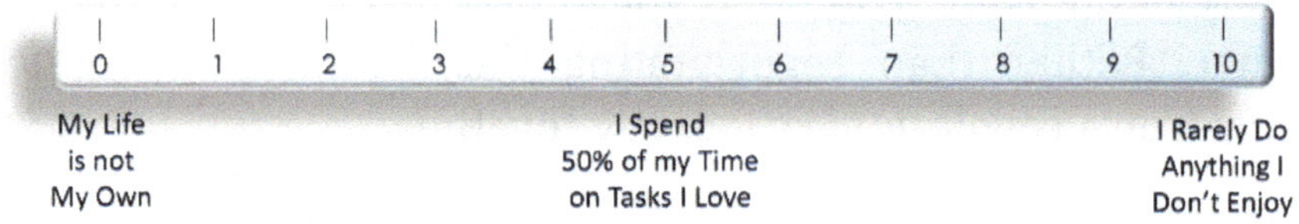

What level of passivity do you choose to reach your life goals?

Passivity Index

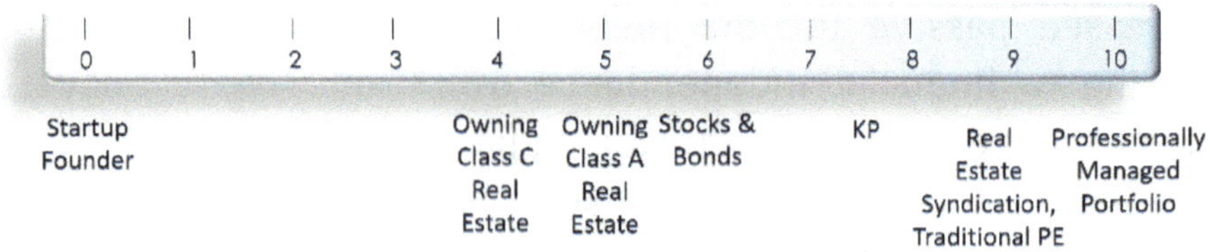

If you score less than eight on a scale of ten for the first two questions, worry not, my friends! It can be difficult to fully own your time early in the journey. The road is long, but the ride is exciting!

Maturing Perspectives on Work

In this book, we are not going to assume that work is something that is bad and that it is something we need to do away with as soon as we are wealthy enough to do so. Work has many benefits, including the stability that comes from a steady paycheck and the feeling that you are doing something valuable or "contributing to society." As your freedom quotient continues to grow, the nature of your work will change as you gain the ability to choose work that you love. You may find that working actively is something that you want to remain a part of your life or something you would like to continue or even return to. You can only come to this realization after you have become work optional. If you become free to have this realization early in your life, at the peak of your abilities, you will have the opportunity to channel this "contribution impulse" into vastly more rewarding tasks.

Most people retire "all at once" at the end of their career only to find that they "no longer feel useful," at which point it is too late to go back. Alternatively, with passive income, you can enjoy "test retirements" of varying intensity as you explore how you and your family react to this new world. If you do decide to break free from the need to work once and for all, you can do it boldly because you have removed the fear of the unknown. If you decide that certain types of work still suit you, the good news is that you haven't burned your bridges yet.

Case in point: your humble author has spent years growing his passive wealth to the point that he doesn't actually need to work. But rather than simply lounging around or constantly traveling, I have found new jobs for myself with the time I have cleared away from the need to work, all while creating abundant new space in my life for my entire family to live more passionately as well. In fact, this very book is evidence of this trend in my life. By leaving the workaday world, I cleared out more space in my life to contribute in ways that I find more meaningful, such as through authoring books and mentorship, while still leaving increased room for my family and personal growth.

Passionate Living is a "Muscle"

Now let's deal with the elephant in the room. There are those who will tell you that the reason that you need to enjoy life now is that you may not make it to that magical number of 65 years of age or that you may finally retire only to find that you are unable to enjoy life's adventure like you did while you were young. They are only half right. The truest reason that you should expand your mind to the lifestyle of the passionate passive investor is that lust for life is like a muscle that grows with exercise. You will begin to see your passion grow like the ripples in a pond. Commit today to living larger than you did yesterday, and you will begin to feel the ripples grow in your life. Before long, you will be helping others throw their own stone in the pond.

If you are wondering whether these methods work, I can start by telling you what they have done for me. In just a few short years, I was able to leave my 9 to 5 behind. I went from being a "recovering Ph.D." and "recovering workaholic" to living life with delicious balance. Now, I eat a late lunch with my kids every day when they come home from school; I send my wife on spa days with her best friend. My family was able to hire help to take care of housekeeping, tutoring, and childcare. Additionally, I lost 40 pounds, became conversational in Spanish in three months, and am training for my first Argentine tango showcase. I have the opportunity to enjoy listening to the waves on my sailboat instead of worrying about what the b-o-s-s thinks. Along the way, I found that my vision continued to grow along with my passive income. Life has become the continuously developing product of an ever-expanding imagination. I will check back in on those spa days and the whirlwind of an early (semi-) retirement in the chapter

"Preparing for the Permanent Vacation," but we will keep things light for now. In the next chapter, I will dive deeper into how I created a lifestyle where my family can "live the dream."

Are you ready? *Let's embark on the journey of a lifetime!*

How I Built My Runway to Financial Freedom

"A mile of road will take you a mile, but a mile of runway can take you anywhere."

- Author Unknown

It was an ordinary day at my desk, consumed by the intricacies of financial predictive models. Months of dedication culminated in a project of my own conception that would later win the company a prestigious award. But the honors and accolades were far in the future. Unfortunately, at the time, my boss didn't see the project in a positive light, and I was about to be demoted for that very same work that would later bring acclaim to the company and myself.

Although I never doubted my ability to put the pieces back together and regain my position, I had no illusions. The road back to where I was before would be long and arduous. As Robin Sharma famously said, "A bad day for the ego is a good day for the soul". Let's just say that this was a very good day for my soul. Finding the goodness in that day took a lot of soul-searching as well as the perspective of time. It forced me to reevaluate priorities, which led me to purchase a small sailboat that produced an abundance of family memories and formed an integral part of our family's journey toward a more fulfilling life.

Shortly before that fateful day, my sister came to me with a plan to start a construction company. As a lover of challenges, the idea immediately appealed to me. Little did I know how soon I would need the runway to financial independence I had been constructing! Although I would remain employed in the same field for nearly half a decade, the quality of that experience was greatly enhanced by the knowledge every morning that even if I had to part ways today, I would be in much stronger shape with cash-flowing assets than most of my neighbors at work.

Before this, my career centered around tech and data science, where I excelled and innovated. However, the allure of entrepreneurship beckoned when my sister proposed a construction venture. The prospect of charting a new course was exhilarating, contrasting sharply with the structured corporate environment. Entrepreneurship fed my appetite for challenge and independence, providing a fresh perspective on work and life.

Balancing my corporate job with entrepreneurial ventures reshaped my lifestyle. Generous vacation time allowed for family outings and personal pursuits, while evenings were devoted to building passive income streams. The flexibility of remote work during the pandemic further fueled my entrepreneurial ambitions, symbolized by our cherished sailboat—a tangible representation of newfound autonomy.

Realizing that there was no loyalty from my employer, I started to enjoy the generous vacation time that went along with my high-paying job. By taking full advantage of weekends, I could still earn six figures while spending 37% of my time on vacation! The family started to go on weekend trips more often, while I learned to use my evening time to build more streams of income. I used the lack of a commute (partially, at first during the pandemic, and fully later on) to invest in my health. Nothing came to symbolize my entrepreneurial journey more closely than the sailboat. I was finally charting my own course in the fullest sense.

As my entrepreneurial endeavors flourished, from construction to apartment ownership and syndications, I diversified my income sources. This strategic approach, blending active and passive investments, gradually eclipsed my corporate earnings. The transition from W-2 employee to financial independence became less daunting, empowering me to embrace change with confidence. As interest rates climbed, so did layoffs in the fintech sector. Prepared by years of planning and partnership, my exit was met with anticipation rather than anxiety.

So, you may wonder, how did that fateful day go? As interest rates climbed at an unprecedented clip, the finance sector needed fewer employees, and the scene I am about to describe is one that was about to unfold countless times over the coming months in the financial industry. I was called into a Friday afternoon videoconference with a half-dozen characters that I didn't see on a daily basis, including one from human resources. It was clear what was going on from the get-go. I just watched the entire surreal scene unfold as if I was watching TV. The people on the call seemed more nervous than me. After all, they had to worry about losing their jobs, I didn't. When the final disclaimer was read to me, I was asked if there was anything I had to say. I said, "Thank you," and that was that. I was a free man!

To understand how the conversation with my wife went, you need to understand that we had been preparing for this for the last five years, so it came as little surprise. She just told me to "pursue my passion," and that was that. We went on to experience some of the most enjoyable times in our lives in the months following the "velvet divorce" from my W-2. For months we enjoyed what to me felt like a "second honeymoon" as we negotiated the changes in our life with a newfound sense of hopefulness and bliss. As I will discuss in "The Zen of Passive Investing," a transition from the workaday world to a world of your own design and a life of your own choosing can be quite a shock. Many couples falter at this stage.

Within three years of departing the corporate world, I achieved personal milestones I previously thought unimaginable. I whipped my body into the best shape of my life, getting down to

19% body fat! To hear the story about how I was able to do this all while eating chocolate every day, you will have to wait for my next book.

Family time also improved. I was able to hug my wife in the late morning and also in the afternoon. I could greet my children when they came home from school and have not just a "family dinner" but a late "family lunch" during the week as well! Not only did physical fitness improve, family time increased, and personal passions like tango flourished. Each day became a canvas for new experiences and personal growth, unencumbered by the demands of a traditional job.

How the Sausage was Made

Each journey from W-2 to financial and time freedom is bound to be unique; however, several principles unite these distinct journeys. Whether you're starting with capital or sweat equity or balancing a W-2 job with side ventures, building multiple income streams is critical. This gradual approach not only mitigates risk but allows for continuous learning and adaptation.

Several factors that will influence your trajectory include how much capital you have to start with, whether you will be amplifying the impact of the capital by adding "sweat" alongside your capital, and whether you will continue to work at a W-2 job while building passive wealth.

Regardless of how you start out, if you want the ride to passive Income nirvana to be "comfortable," you will certainly want to build multiple streams of income to avoid "putting all of your eggs in one basket." Whether that means multiple operating businesses, several apartments, private loans, private equity, or (ideally) some combination thereof, is up to you. Taking your time to progressively build your basket of passive income producing investments has several advantages. Not only does this provide you the time to continue to educate yourself throughout your course of investment, but it also gives you some time to see how well your investments with different operators "perform" as you experience "exits" throughout your journey.

Taking steady, progressive action in building your runway to financial and time freedom is essential to your mental health. Unless you have a high tolerance for pain, don't try to do it all at once by quitting your job and going "full time" as an investor. As I will explore in later chapters, the same holds true for exploring retirement. There are distinct advantages to a progressive approach, namely that you remain in control of the process. By remaining in control, you will have the time to plan, pivot, and adapt rather than being driven by circumstances.

I will share with you just a few brief highlights from my personal journey, your mileage may vary. In 2016, my family founded a residential construction company. For the next six years, I continued to work at my W-2 job while continuing to build my business and investing acumen. By 2020, I had become an apartment owner and private lender. My first (and third and sixth) apartments were purchased with seller financing, which means that you don't need to have a ton of money or a "track record" to get started. In 2021, I made my first passive real estate investment in an apartment syndication, and I joined two other syndications as an active investor. I experienced my first "exit" as a passive investor and made my first private equity investment and angel investment in 2022, the same year that I made an "exit" from my W-2. Leaving the workaday world not only gave me the time to go "all in" as an investor but also allowed me to become a "real estate professional," an event that brought profoundly positive tax implications. In 2023, I refinanced my first apartment with agency debt, providing a great deal of liquidity. The family construction company will complete its first subdivision in 2024. At the time of this writing, I look forward to a future of boundless growth both as an investor and as a human.

In the next chapter, we'll delve deeper into constructing your runway to passionate living. Whether you're on the brink of retirement or just beginning, I'll guide you in living passionately within your current means. By reframing work as a choice and integrating financial freedom into a balanced life, we'll uncover the joy of pursuing what truly matters.

Now, Your Journey

I will explore "passionate living" and develop your game plan in detail in a later chapter. For now, I just want to give you a taste of what passionate living may look like in your life and to introduce the idea of freedom being an upwards spiraling journey rather than a destination that you hope to reach "someday" and then hope that you can figure out what to do when you get there. We can start small (remember I told you that my sailboat is *small*). I bought it for $5,000 and yet it was big enough for my entire family of four. You *can* start traveling now (and enjoying your local surroundings more, too) on your current budget. As you build passive income, your time freedom, and means will only amplify your ability to live life's adventure to the full. But enough of the fun stuff for now. We need to get back to the nuts and bolts!

How to Start Building Your Runway Even if You Aren't Ready to Quit Your Job

Without the security provided by the multiple streams of passive (and active) income that I built; I would have never had the opportunity to seize the opportunity to fully pursue my passions. One crucial lesson here is the importance of starting early on your financial runway, long before you plan to depart full-time employment. Starting small and diversifying your investments is key to weathering economic storms and learning valuable lessons without risking everything on a single venture.

Taking Action

Taking action now is crucial. Reflect on past setbacks; they can be powerful motivators for resilience and growth. If you feel you could have handled past challenges better, use them as fuel to strengthen your resolve.

Imagine a life liberated from current constraints. Picture having passive income flowing in regularly, freeing you from the Monday morning grind. Don't worry if you're skeptical about achieving this; for now, focus on visualizing what such a life could look like. Would you spend more time with family, pursue new ventures, or delve into personal hobbies? Dare to envision a life filled with possibilities.

Would you spend more time with your children or grandchildren, would you launch a new company, or would you just enjoy a new hobby? Would you get into the best shape of your life? Literally, anything that is achievable in human life is achievable in your life. If you are not imagining something amazing right now, you aren't trying hard enough.

Living The Dream!

"Success is doing what you want to do, when you want, where you want, with whom you want, as much as you want."

- Tony Robbins

My life of fearing no one and being free to embark on any adventure that tickles my fancy in real time was a journey, not a destination. In life, I do this thing called "what I want," and there is no reason that you can't do the same! Now that we have covered my journey to passionate living success in the last chapter. It is time to help you build your own personalized plan that allows you to do the same.

Imagine living the life of your dreams without having to grind it out at the office from 9 to 5 every week. Consider what it would be like to hear about an exotic destination and have the freedom to just "pick up and go" without having to ask. Does that sound too good to be true? Unlike one of those slimy "get rich quick" books, this is no fairy tale. This book takes a different approach. We are going to take a step-by-step approach that will, if followed rigorously, lead to personal growth and fulfillment, at least as important as the wealth we are going to build together.

Before you order that Lamborghini from the local dealership, let's define our terms to make sure we are on the same page. "Passive income" is money that you have coming in regularly, regardless of whether you continue to work or not. It is literally like getting paid to breathe. Once you have enough passive money coming in that doesn't require you to continue "turning the crank" to receive it, you will have attained a state known as "financial freedom" where you get to spend your time wherever you like, with whomever you choose.

As I will see, "passive" doesn't mean easy. You may have to work a great deal to create a passive stream of income in the first place if you aren't already. But don't worry about that yet. I will show you how you can put your money to work to compound returns and grow over time. I will also provide you with the tools you need to track your progress towards this enlightened state of living.

However, if you expect a book (even this particularly fine book that you, gentle reader, presently hold in your discerning hands) to change your life, you will be disappointed. There is a reason that most people aren't wealthy. It is because the discipline that it takes to build, maintain, and enjoy wealth is not easy. The road ahead is not easy, but I assure you that the prize will be worth the price you pay. If you are eager for a brief glimpse of what I envision, flip to the final chapter, "Arete."

Let's consider the Tony Robbins quote from the chapter heading anew and ask yourself, "How hard am I willing to *work* to make that dream a reality?".

But I don't just want you to just do *well* as an investor. I want to see you *crush it.* This book is here to introduce you to the wide world of private markets, which will allow you to enjoy outsized returns. Ordinary approaches produce ordinary results. *Extraordinary* results require going beyond what 95% of people are willing to do. Just building a working understanding of the various asset classes available in private markets puts you significantly ahead of the game. I will also discuss other great (often unseen) opportunities like using a self-directed IRA that puts you in charge of your investing future by allowing you to invest in each of the alternative assets I talk about in this book.

The Three Pillars

This approach to wealth building can be divided into three cardinal ideas.

Pillar I: Capitalize on Hidden Opportunities

First, we will avail ourselves of opportunities that most people miss, like investing in private markets and using a self-directed IRA. It is hard to find above-average opportunities if you are looking in the same places everyone else is.

Second, to maximize our ability to find hidden opportunities, our goal is to keep our eyes wide open as humble seekers of truth and wisdom. No matter how much we "know" about the investing world, the ideal asset class or the ideal tax strategy will change as the world (and tax laws) change. By keeping an open mind as a seeker of knowledge, rather than allowing ourselves to think of ourselves as "experts," we, like the kōan of the teacup (see "The Zen of Passive Investing"), retain enough space to grow our knowledge and experience as we adapt to the ever-changing investment landscape.

Pillar II: Take Immediate and Massive Action

Tomorrow is a lie! We aren't going to put off making improvements in our investments or personal development. Immediate action, no matter how small, cements your commitment to tackling a new opportunity or reaching a desired goal. Reaching any significant goal requires excellence - and excellence is a *habit*. Whatever value you squeeze out any new approach is likely to be found in what you apply more or less immediately; it is important to start building habits before you forget or move on to other projects. Give it your all, then decide later what to keep and throw away

A commitment to taking immediate action is not an excuse to act in a precipitous fashion. For example, you may not be able to find the next key deal or master the rules of success in a new asset class. Consider how the chess master approaches the game. It seems that he is doing nothing for long periods, but nothing could be farther from the truth. A chess master is always thinking five, seven, or ten moves ahead, sometimes more. Don't beat yourself up if you haven't made a "move" recently. Focus on the quality of the move you are preparing.

It is important to commit not only to immediate action but also to *massive* action. If you decide that you can't make a "move" today and that you must focus on self-education or planning, how massive can you make that action? How many pages will you read this afternoon? How many podcasts will you listen to this evening? And if it is planning that you are focused on, how deeply are you planning? Are you hashing and rehashing the same scenarios without adding additional information? Or are you employing spreadsheets and forecasting tools or building your own tools to answer the question of where to move next?

Not knowing "enough" or not having your "plan" sufficiently together to act can be an excuse. Analysis can lead to paralysis. You need to be the final judge of whether your learning and planning is an excuse for inaction. One way to test yourself to see whether you are delaying action for the right reasons is to observe the nature and quality of your preparations. Are you hungrily consuming knowledge? Does each fact or preparation bring you closer to your goal? Have your preparations precisely focused and sharpened your plan of action? Or are you aimlessly passing time without coming closer to executing your course of action?

Few people who focus like a laser beam come to failure. If you use your time to focus your investing approach on a hunting ground of manageable size, you will quickly bag your quarry or conclude that more fertile hunting grounds exist elsewhere. Alternately, it is the investor that is simply looking for "a good deal" who finds it impossible to come to a conclusion as to whether it makes sense to "pull the trigger". It is impossible to know whether this apple or that orange represents the best opportunity if you aren't clear on what you are looking for. You need to know whether you are looking for apples or oranges so that you can learn to spot the lemons. The risk of total inaction without a narrow focus is too great. Focus, and win. Only then try another course of action.

Pillar III: Continuous, qualitative, iterative improvement:

I will ensure that the impact of our efforts is multiplied by seeking continuous, qualitative, iterative improvement. Version one beats version none - *every time*. Take a step towards financial freedom today and every day. Make sure that you aren't just "executing". If you only play out your old game plan each day, you aren't really getting better. The world will change and leave you behind. I know that I just told you to "focus like a laser beam." But that doesn't mean that you can't take 5% or even 10% of your professional time to "sharpen the saw." If you are a bond investor, study quantitative analysis to deepen your investment acumen. If you invest in stocks, read books on financial statement analysis. If you invest in private equity, sharpen your underwriting acumen. A day that passes without sharpening a valuable skill is a day wasted as an investor. To reach your goals, you need to grow qualitatively as an investor (and in life).

Even if the first step to growing your skills or acumen is to read one chapter of this book every day or to watch ten YouTube videos about wealth creation - do it! Don't disparage a step as "too small" or let someone moving faster bring you down. Wealth building is a race much longer than the Kentucky Derby. Even in a short race, the horses never seem to end up in the same order at the beginning, middle, and then again at the end of the race. The person urging you to go faster than you feel appropriate at this time may flame out miserably. When markets are rising, the advice from gurus is to just "find a deal." How many of those gurus will survive the next recession? Focus on what you do best. Stay in your lane. Run your own race.

Focus on both quantitative as well as qualitative gains. If you improve just 1% each day, you will win big! Spoiler alert: you can't always improve 1% every day quantitatively. Imagine running 1% faster each day. You will be Usain Bolt in no time. Unfortunately, it just doesn't work that way. Quantitative gains are important, but quantitative gains alone won't take you there. You will need to make many qualitative improvements along the way to run faster. Consider a sprinter trying to improve each day. Here are some ideas for qualitative gains. Get some coaching. Improve your gait by taking smaller steps. Engage your core as you focus on dynamic balance. Focus on strength training. Learn how to pump your arms more aerodynamically to drive you forward more efficiently. Try running against a grade to increase the challenge. Learn to breathe in synch with your gait to avoid wasted energy. Learn pacing. Focus on mindset. Even something (seemingly) as simple as running on a track between two white lines is full of complexity. You don't get there on a linear path (even if you are a sprinter).

Alternatively, consider the high jump. Early high jumpers looked much like hurdlers clearing the bar feet first. Over time, the original techniques became "played out," and further gains could only be found by a more sideways-horizontal approach. I will spare you the gory details of the Eastern Cut-off, the Western Roll, and the Straddle. A technique that had its world debut in Mexico in the year 1968 supplanted them all. It was there that Dick Fosbury cleared the bar headfirst with his back to the bar. The Fosbury flop, as it became known, is the technique that has become the staple of the sport ever since. Even if you never become the innovator that drives a field forward with an entirely new approach, to grow personally, you need to look for these opportunities in your own approach to business, investing, and life.

You can't jump directly from where you are to where you want to be. It is not possible to find your first (or next big investment) today. But if you commit to taking the biggest (rational) step each day, you can grow into your dream quickly (and your dream will grow too!)

This approach is not just for making gains in business and investing but for life as well. Each investment you make in living larger will contribute to your imagination, which will help you...live larger still! Spiral up to a life you never imagined you could live!

Laying the Foundation for Your New Life

If you're still reading, now is the time to take your first step towards a new life. Have you committed to at least one act of passionate living, something you wouldn't have considered before picking up this book? Take action today, before you go to sleep — *throw that stone into the pond of possibility!*

The Three Pillars of Passionate Living Through Passive Investing These pillars distill the various strategies and wisdom I have garnered through my climb to the top of the greasy pole of financial independence and individual freedom into three principal approaches. Use them to organize your journey!

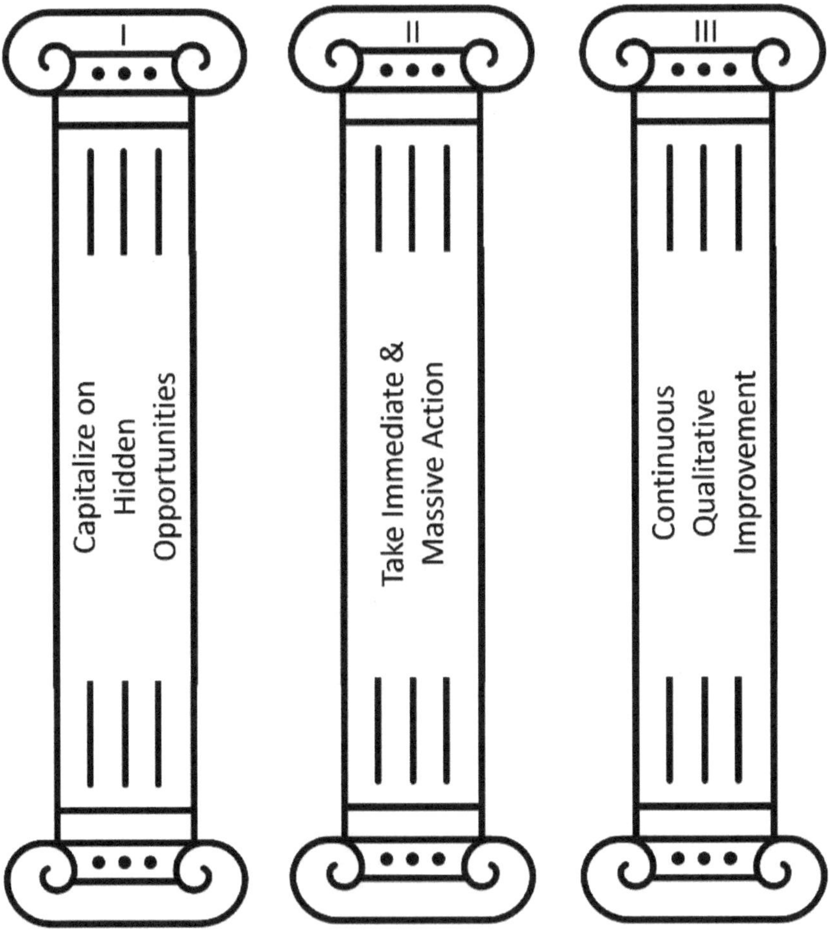

Dream, Believe, Achieve!

"Commitment is what transforms a promise into a reality... Commitment is the stuff character is made of; the power to change the face of things. It is the daily triumph of integrity over skepticism."

- Abraham Lincoln

We need to define "dream life" a bit more precisely before the dream becomes real enough to turn into a plan. The first step is to create a compelling vision for your life. The success of a lifetime can hinge on a single moment. This very moment can be the pivotal moment of your life. Challenge yourself to imagine a life that isn't just quantitatively better (more money, losing a few pounds, having a little more time to do the things we want to do). Instead, try imagining a life that is *qualitatively* different from your life at present. Instead of imagining more of your current good life, imagine yourself doing things you never imagined with people you haven't even met yet because you took control of your financial future today and found out just how sweet life can be.

Dream, Believe, Achieve

Take a moment to imagine your dream life. A life of your choosing. A life where you direct the action *and* play the starring role. What would you do, where would you be, and who would you be enjoying this amazing life with? Fill in the following blanks for a tangible reminder you can use every day to keep you on track for real estate wealth!

Where: *I would like to be in* ______________________ *right now.*

Who: *I would have more time to spend with* ______________.

What: *I would finally have time to* ______________________.

Now, for extra credit, draw a picture of what your dream life would look like. It's OK if you want to just close your eyes and imagine.

Ok – pencils down! -

Who drew a sailboat? (extra points if you did, *yours truly* loves to sail).

Whatever you drew, this is *your* unique dream. This is the life that you truly deserve, and using the methods in this book, we are going to achieve that dream.

But, before you can seriously get to work on this dream, you need to actually *believe* that you can make your dream a reality. Instead of telling yourself, "I am wealthy," "I live in a mansion," "My pockets are already full of money. I can hardly close my wallet. I will find a $100 bill in my pocket next time I do the laundry." or "I am a social butterfly, and every desirable member of the opposite sex wants to take me out to the finest steakhouse in town this Saturday," try instead to convince yourself that you have the discipline and consistency to fully commit to your goal and *win*. Gentle reader, you have really big goals, if you didn't, you probably would have put this book down by now. Big goals require big commitments to realize. To build that sort of commitment, we need something more believable. Something that you can say to yourself and actually mean. If you don't truly believe it, your subconscious mind won't do the work to make it happen. Pretending that you already have what you seek may short-circuit your motivation to make it happen. We don't want to stifle your motivation; we want to increase your appetite for success! If you have tried affirmations before, and they didn't change your life, you are not alone. It's OK to admit it - it's not your fault!

An Affirmitment, not an Affirmation

Affirmations are designed to encourage you and help you believe that you can reach your goals. This can be good if you are experiencing some distortion of reality, such as feeling "fat" despite maintaining a healthy weight or feeling unsuccessful despite significant accomplishments. If this accurately describes you, then by all means, you should be using affirmations to help adjust your self-image to reality. Tell yourself, "I am beautiful, and I am worthy," or "I am effective and have a solid track record that others would envy." When it comes to "being," affirmations can be helpful.

However, affirmations lead you to visualize yourself as already having reached the goal or already possessing the desired character trait. Visualizing yourself as already being in an ideal state can rob you of the motivation to reach that state. Let's admit it. You don't fully believe the affirmations you repeat about the future. When we are interested in "becoming," I reach for something stronger.

Believing in your dream is essential. Instead of merely affirming wealth or success, focus on building a deep-seated belief in your ability to achieve your goals. Craft an "affirmmitment" that resonates with your values and aspirations. Motivation is worthless the moment it starts to rain. Let's make a plan that is designed to work, rain or shine.

Reframe your Goal as an Affirmitment

"I will achieve my goal of _________. because I am willing to do whatever it takes to overcome the obstacles in my way. I commit to the following daily actions ________ that align with my vision because ______________ means too much to me to give up."

Personalizing your affirmmitment ensures your commitment is rooted in authenticity and purpose, driving sustained effort and progress.

Wow, that was a mouthful! I highly suggest that you fundamentally modify the above script to suit your goals and your personality. Make sure that you keep the elements of discipline and commitment front and center in your affirmmitment. It will make all the difference in the world in your ability to take decisive action. This program is not about "waiting for Godot." It is about leaving behind all the limiting beliefs that have prevented you from reaching your dream *today*. Don't kid yourself, these limiting beliefs will be back. But don't worry, I will provide you with the tools you need to smash these limiting beliefs a thousand times if need be. Each time, that voice of limitation will get a little smaller, and the new you will get louder. I will have to work at keeping the dream alive. And the dream *is* alive, as long as your commitment is greater than your fear. Have you ever wondered why that last motivational speaker that you believed in failed to change your life? It's because you only believed that change was possible until life happened and rained on your plan. Did you make a second plan or a third plan and keep executing? Did you pivot when the first idea didn't work? If you are like most people, you didn't. And that's why you were left with only platitudes and "feel good" phrases from your motivational speaker encounter.

What does your financial freedom look like?

By going beyond a simple affirmation and committing ourselves to discipline and consistency, we have already taken the first step toward our goal by creating something believable. You may still not fully believe that your goal is reachable. I can feel it. This may be too touchy-feely for you, and if that's the case, it's OK. You are about to see that this program of personal growth is all about eating your peas and spinach. For some, you may still be stuck in thinking that this is another "get rich quick" scheme and you may want to put the book down. Rest assured that this is a "get rich slowly and consistently" approach. I want you to reach your goal of your dream lifestyle far more than I want to sell you a book. If you truly believe that "the juice is worth the squeeze," you will stay on the path to wealth long enough to taste the freedom that only financial independence can produce.

Why Motivation Isn't Enough

Motivation is great when you feel it. The problem is what to do when you don't. This is where drive and commitment come in. Motivation wanes, especially in the face of challenges. True commitment, however, endures. As David Goggins aptly puts it, "Motivation comes and goes. When you are driven, everything in front of you gets destroyed." Embrace drive over motivation to sustain your journey. Desire lights the fire, but determination sees you through.

Accountability Partner

As Rudyard Kipling aptly put it, "For the strength of the pack is the wolf, and the strength of the wolf is the pack." And so it is with accountability. To significantly increase your chances of success, find an accountability partner. This could be a friend, coach, or colleague who supports and challenges you to stay on track with your goals. Accountability partners provide essential feedback and encouragement and also ensure you stay committed even when motivation ebbs.

Consider different types of accountability partners:

- **Task-oriented**: Ensures you complete specific actions.
- **Camaraderie**: Provides mutual support, like a gym buddy.
- **Emotional support**: Helps navigate emotional barriers and setbacks.
- **Aspirational**: Inspires you to think bigger and challenge limiting beliefs.

Choose a partner who aligns with your needs and goals. This will enhance your commitment and progress towards your dream lifestyle.

An accountability partner may be someone that you formally choose such as a coach or a friend with which you have weekly calls to track your progress versus your goals. More commonly, your accountability partner is someone with whom you are already close but may not yet realize as such. If you are an entrepreneur, your team members are your accountability partners because you know that they and their families are counting on you, and you don't want to let them down. If you have a friend who notices when you are slipping on your commitment to diet and fitness and is able to call you back to your commitment in a loving way, you already have an accountability partner. If you have a friend that you go to the gym with or a business partner, you have an instant accountability partner.

Before you dismiss the idea of an accountability partner as a "hassle" or an inconvenience, consider that you could have some uncomfortable conversations now and enjoy a greatly enhanced likelihood of success, or go it alone and potentially face a preventable failure. Accountability partners come at various levels, from the task-oriented to the inspirational. Depending on where you are in your commitment to your goals, there is going to be the right type of accountability partner for you, from the task-oriented to the aspirational. If your accountability partner isn't making a huge impact or seems to be a "pain," you have probably picked an accountability partner at the wrong level.

Just as accountability partners come in many levels, they also come in two flavors. The aforementioned coach is an "accountability provider" and represents a one-way relationship accountability partner where they provide, and you receive. Ideally, you should find an accountability relationship where you provide mutual value for the deepest return on effort. There is nothing wrong with using a coach as your ready-made accountability partner, just don't stop there.

It could be someone who calls you each week to see if you completed the tasks you committed to, I (lovingly) refer to this type of accountability partner as a "box checker" or a "nag."

There is nothing wrong if this is what you need where you are at, just don't stay there for long. At a slightly higher level, we have the "camaraderie partner," who is someone like your gym mate. Next up, we encounter the "emotional support" commitment partner. This is the friend who lovingly reminds you of your commitment to fitness and makes you actually want the six-pack abs more than the macaroon, leaving you feeling reenergized and connected to your dreams. A friend may be uniquely qualified to take the time to explore your emotions and conflicts and help you figure out why you let yourself down. Finally, I will consider the aspirational commitment partner. This is probably a colleague that you interact with regularly and who inspires you. This is the person who helps you crush your limiting beliefs and see the opportunity in every challenge.

In the final analysis, the best accountability partner can only do so much. The choice is yours. The work and the glory are yours for the taking.

Types of Accountability Partners Accountability partners vary in the intensity of the accountability as well as the intensity of the amount of "love" that they bring to the relationship. If you feel that an accountability relationship isn't powerful enough and that you can "check-in" on your own tasks, consider moving up the accountability chain toward a more aspirational partner.

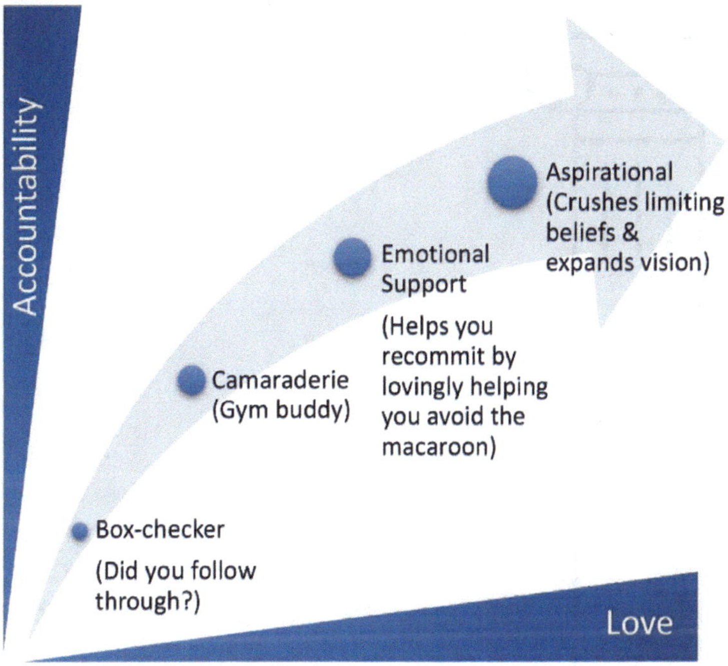

Pillar I – Capitalize on Unseen Opportunities The journey so far has provided an overview of the terrain ahead. Next, we will focus on Pillar I – Capitalize on Unseen Opportunities over the next two chapters. We are about to open our eyes to the exciting world of private markets and the opportunities they have to offer.

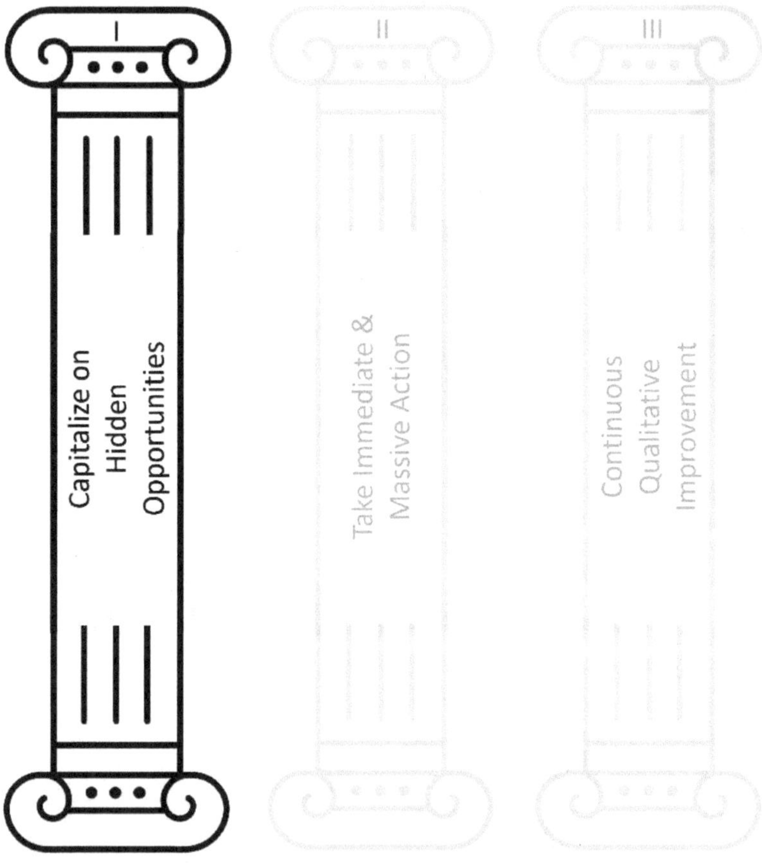

Your Passive Income Playbook: A World of Opportunity

"Blessed are the curious, for they shall have adventures."

- Lovelle Drachman

Dear passive income, how can I find thee? Let me count the ways (with apologies to Elizabeth Barrett Browning). Passive income comes in many forms, each as unique as the individuals who seek it. I will explore as many possibilities as I can pack in. Each of the following categories could spawn a book (or series of books) on their own. The following is meant simply as a jumping-off point. Although we are focused on passive investing here, it is important to understand value-add strategies to help you evaluate deal quality. Accordingly, I will discuss the basic details of operating these investments so that you are prepared to fully evaluate the opportunities that cross your desk.

In this chapter, I will take a wide view of passive investing. Rather than limiting ourselves to passive income (which is important, and which is what you will ultimately need to keep the party going), I will cast a wider net by including all sorts of passive investments, regardless of whether they produce a steady stream of income or whether they happen to be more growth-focused or even defensive in nature. Although I will mention investments available in public markets (for example, stocks and bonds), I will focus on private markets for the breadth of opportunities offered.

I have personally invested in many of the following asset classes, which have contributed to my current lifestyle through the expansion of my wealth as well as through providing the benefits of diversification. One of the great things about investing passively is that you don't need to be nearly as expert as operators in the field to evaluate and make sound investments. This allows you to have your "fingers in many pots," so to speak. Learning is an important part of the passive investing journey. If you love to learn, you will find that passive investing provides you with never-ending opportunities to build your business acumen. Details on the operation and value-add approaches for various asset classes are included to help the reader evaluate the business plans that you will encounter throughout your passive investing career.

Because the wide world of passive investing is so broad, I have broken this chapter down into five sections, namely I. real estate and syndications, II. private lending, III. private equity, angel, and venture capital IV. operating businesses, and V. stocks, bonds, and "other." I would recommend picking one or a few of the following asset classes that suit you and your cash flow needs to start with and then expand slowly from there. There is no reason to stay on the first passive investing square that you land on. Happy investing, my friends!

Section I. Real Estate and Syndications

Multifamily (Apartment) Syndications

Investing in multifamily provides stability in a constantly changing market. By investing in apartments, you are providing a basic need. Unless we all end up deciding to live in a tent out in the woods, housing will continue to be a major industry in the US. Apartment syndications can often produce returns at least as strong as the stock market while avoiding much of the stock market's volatility. Syndication allows you to invest with others, spreading risk while benefiting from professional management.

Most people assume that they aren't wealthy enough to invest in apartments. Through syndication, in which multiple investors come together to make an investment that none of the investors could have made on their own, you can find yourself invested passively in real estate for a minimum investment of around $50,000. In syndication, the management duties are handled by the general partnership team, making real estate a truly passive investment. This leaves you, the limited partner, free to focus on the things you love.

By investing your money in multifamily, you are investing in one of the safest, growing assets in America today - housing. Unlike office space, which has undergone a surprising if not shocking contraction in recent years, housing is an absolute necessity, something we simply can't do without. Although there is nothing that can *guarantee* a return on investment, housing is one of the more stable asset classes on the market. Real estate also produces significant cash flow because (all together now, class) – the rent is always due! This cash flow can be a great way to fund your lifestyle because it doesn't require you to burn your principal.

Delaware Statutory Trusts (DST)

From the standpoint of the passive investor, a DST is highly similar to a syndication. You get all of the benefits of being a passive investor in a syndication with the additional benefit that you can use a 1031 exchange into and out of a DST; a fact which can have profound benefits on your wealth accumulation, as we will see later in the chapter "Protecting Your Wealth."

Significant differences between a DST and a syndication that you should be aware of include a higher minimum investment which is usually $100,000. Also, you will need to be accredited to invest. DST investments tend to focus on portfolios of large, high-quality institutional-grade assets meaning that your expected returns may not be as high as with syndication but will hopefully be "smoother" over the long run. You will also have to consider broker fees with a DST which can range from a flat fee to as high as 5% to 10%. To put it in perspective, remember that these fees are almost certainly less than you would pay in taxes.

Retail

That strip mall on the corner may also be a great investment. One of the most exciting things about investing in retail is the fact that often, the tenant pays for the taxes, insurance, utilities, as well as maintenance! Since your profit is net of the above three big-ticket items, these leases are referred to as "triple-net" or "NNN" leases for short. The regularity of income and the ease of operations make triple-net properties great to own!

Since the tenants sign long-term leases and take care of the day-to-day maintenance, this is one type of real estate that you, as a (somewhat) passive investor, can invest directly in. The steady cash flow from NNN properties leads to a natural analogy between a NNN investment and a bond.

Office Space

Owners of office buildings have certainly taken a beating since the pandemic. If your investment thesis focuses on investing where there is "blood in the streets," then offices may be for you. However, as the pandemic demonstrated, offices are not an absolute necessity and are nowhere near as important as they were once perceived to be. In an opportunistic asset class, events move quickly. You will want to be sure that you have an up-to-the-minute understanding of the market. At the time of publication, class-A office space has been doing better than lower-quality buildings. Like any asset class you consider investing in, you will have to do a fair amount of research to get a handle on what assets make the most sense at a given time. Like retail, office space often provides the owner with the ease of NNN leases.

Industrial

There are several subclasses of industrial, including factories, data centers, flex space, distribution warehouses, and cold storage, just to name a few. Owning industrial space can be lucrative due to the barriers to entry for new investors, which limits competition. For starters, the aspects of an industrial property that make it attractive to tenants may seem arcane upon first blush. For example, the suitability of a particular space for a tenant may depend on various factors, including clear heights (important for distribution centers), loading docks, and rail service (important for heavy industry). As with retail, cash flows can easily dry up for an extended period upon the loss of a tenant.

Generally, industrial tenants will sign a NNN lease which, in principle, makes this a passive income asset class. If you decide to invest in industrial real estate, make sure that you have the financial wherewithal to handle vacancies. If an economic downturn comes, and you need to renegotiate your lease to keep your tenant, or worse yet, lose them altogether, you need to be sure that you will be able to cover the expenses of a vacant building until you can find another tenant, which may be years. Also, remember that when you do find a tenant, your troubles are not over yet. Just like office and retail, the lease generally requires the landlord to make significant renovations before the new tenant will move in.

Self-Storage

People love their "stuff" - that's one thing that will never change. Most people would rather do anything (including paying another monthly rent check) just to avoid the trouble of having to throw out, give away, or sell the items they have accumulated over a lifetime. An unwillingness to "let go" of inanimate objects may not be a sign of emotional strength, but it does lend a degree of recession resistance to self-storage which is something that definitely warms my heart.

Senior Housing

The "silver tsunami" is real. Every day, 10,000 Americans turn 65. Investing in senior housing is a great way to serve a definite need while funding your retirement portfolio. As an investor in senior housing, you will want to become intimately acquainted with the various levels of service provided, which range from 55+ (active adult), which provide no services onsite, to assisted living, memory care, and finally, nursing homes, which provide the greatest degree of care. Another option to investigate is residential assisted living, which provides high-end care to patients for premium prices.

Key Principal

You can participate in syndications and other financed transactions as a loan guarantor, also known as a key principal or KP for short. To qualify, you will generally need a net worth equal to the loan amount and liquid wealth equal to 10% of the loan amount. You may receive a 10% to 20% share of the general partnership of a syndication as a KP.

You will need to be careful about the character of the operators, the cash flow, and whether the loan is recourse or nonrecourse before signing. Even a nonrecourse loan can become recourse if any of the partners trigger one of the "bad boy carveouts" in the loan document. Some common carveouts include fraud, not paying taxes, bankruptcy, etc. Finally, you need to realize that it is not just your money, but your reputation is on the line each time you sign a loan. If even one lender is not repaid in full, your ability to sign on loans in the future will be jeopardized.

Section II. Private Lending

Owning debt positions provides a buffer against equity volatility. To safeguard your investment, ensure that you take protective measures like securing the first lien position and maintaining prudent lending ratios. A common rule of hard money lenders is to limit the loan size to 65% of the after-repair value (ARV) Releasing money for construction in stages through draws rather than all at once provides protection against borrowers using cash to fund other projects and also from cost overruns.

Gap Lending

When a real estate transaction lacks the funds to get "across the finish line" on time, the general partners in the deal are very hungry for funding at any price. Solving the partners' problem comes at a price, of course. Between the loan fees (aka "points") and the short loan terms, which can often be as short as three months, the effective interest rate can be quite high.

Merchant Cash Advances

Suppose that "Giuseppe's Pizza and Ravioli Restaurant" wants to expand to new locations, or sorely needs to replace a defunct pizza oven but lacks the capital to do so. Guiseppe can collateralize his future revenue to borrow the much-needed cash.

You need to realize that your loan is "collateralized" only by the future revenue stream. If the business fails, you will be left with nothing because the loan isn't backed up by so much as a (crusty) pizza oven.

<u>Section III</u>. Private Equity, Venture, and Angel Investing

Private Equity

Private equity is a broad asset class encompassing a variety of strategies, from growth equity to distressed assets, which offer varied risk profiles. Growth equity involves buying solid companies with a solid earnings history that just need capital to grow to distressed private equity which focuses on "deep value" companies that are currently experiencing difficulties. Depending on your financial situation and goals, you should be able to find a subclass of private equity that suits your level of risk tolerance. If you are looking for high returns and can tolerate a non-cash-flowing asset with an investment horizon of approximately five years, private equity can be an exciting place to invest.

Private equity deals tend to use a great deal of leverage to amplify returns. This is why you will forever see many private equity deals "blow up" when rates increase rapidly. This "financial engineering" leads to great risk not only during the hold period but also after disposition as long as the companies continue to hold the debt.

Angel Investing

If you have ever watched "Shark Tank" and thought to yourself about how exciting it would be to invest in startups, it's - well...different. If you want to invest in early-stage companies, you need to learn to say "no"– a lot. Whereas a typical segment of Shark Tank runs 7 to 12 minutes in duration, the due diligence required before pulling the trigger could easily run anywhere between 40 and 200 hours. That and much else is hidden "behind the scenes."

The amount of effort (and discipline) that goes into making successful seed-stage investments is simply beyond all but the full-time professional angel investor. For this reason, finding a local angel group is paramount for new angel investors. A solid quality group will support you through sourcing deals, performing and providing documentation of due diligence, drawing up legal documents, and most importantly, saying "no" to the vast majority of pitches (that's the discipline part).

Research on angel investing returns indicates that roughly 3 out of 5 angel investments result in a loss. The high returns that come from angel investing come from the roughly 1 in 5 investments that exhibit greater than 2x exits[1]. To ensure high returns in the range of 27% as calculated in studies of angel investors, you will need to diversify and make your investments through a credible angel investment group and either make a large number of investments or invest in a fund. Studies of angel investors identify their sample population through angel investment groups. Individual investors choosing not to invest in a syndicate are likely to experience far less favorable outcomes.

---

[1] DeGennaro, Ramon P., Angel Investors and their Investments (December 1, 2010). Available at SSRN: https://ssrn.com/abstract=1784489

Venture Capital

Venture capital provides a bridge between seed funding and the public markets. The most common way to gain exposure to venture capital is through a fund. Despite the fact that venture capitalists invest in companies that are significantly further along in their growth and development, the likelihood of loss in a single company is similar to angel investing. However, if you are investing in a fund, the law of large numbers is in your favor, and the likelihood of receiving solid returns is high. On the downside, you can't expect any cash flow from angel or venture capital investing, so you will need to balance your portfolio with liquid or cash-flowing assets.

Section IV. Operating Businesses

Franchises

Franchises can be purchased through brokers, which in addition to making the acquisition smoother and more "passive," affords the investor the benefit of the broker's counsel in choosing a business that fits your comfort zone in terms of passivity. If you are willing to do some upfront work on finding the business you want to purchase, you can explore becoming a silent partner in an operating business.

Franchises offer varying levels of involvement, from hands-on management to passive ownership. Certain businesses may require you to step in and run operations until you can promote or recruit a high-quality manager who can take your place in businesses where you may be able to hire a professional manager right off the bat. Warren Buffet only buys businesses in which he trusts that the current management is "competent and honest." Thereafter, he only has to provide oversight. As CEO of the seventh largest company in the US, Warren Buffet is hardly a "passive" investor. You can be sure that he didn't get to where he is today by micromanaging.

Drop Shipping

If you want to buy into a passive business, drop shipping provides a light to moderately capital-intensive option with potential scalability. In such an arrangement, the investor supplies the startup and working capital for an operator who will purchase and warehouse the goods, put up an electronic storefront, and then ship the goods from the warehouse as necessary. Capital needs involve not simply the cost of the warehouse and the replenishment of the goods, but also the need to stock the warehouse with new items as old items become less popular and need to be sold at bargain prices.

Section V. Stocks Bonds, and Other Investments

Stocks (Equities)

For reasonably high returns with high liquidity, equities can't be beaten. No matter how excited you may get about your preferred asset class, make sure that you always include a proper mix of cash and liquid assets to carry you through volatile periods.

Just because stocks have no sophistication or accreditation hurdle doesn't mean that you can afford to be sloppy in your selection criteria. You will need to do careful research into company fundamentals before you invest. On the most basic level, this would include reading and understanding company financial statements. For some great references that will detail what it takes to be a great equities investor, try "The Intelligent Investor" by Benjamin Graham or "Securities Analysis" by Benjamin Graham and David Dodd.

If you don't put in the time, be prepared to join the ranks of the underperformers. If you want to invest in equities, but don't want to put in the time to read financial statements, you would be strongly advised to heed Warren Buffett's advice, namely that "most investors should put their money in a low-cost S&P 500 index fund."

Bonds

Bonds, often overlooked for excitement, offer stability and income potential across diverse markets." Although the simplistic approach of focusing only on US Treasuries may tend to greatly underperform the market, a willingness to explore a variety of government and private issues across both foreign and domestic markets can produce some solid gains. If you are able to build information asymmetry in your favor, you can find bonds trading at a larger discount to par than is merited by the facts. Such an approach can reap strong dividends for the patient investor.

Song Royalties

A desire to acquire assets that are resistant to downturns has led large private equity companies to purchase the music catalogs of famous acts, including Bob Dylan, Kiss, and ZZ Top. The ideal target is an artist with "timeless" appeal. To get a piece of the action, look for a royalty fund. These funds offer not only stability but also high yields, which often range from 8% to 15%.

Creating Your Own Royalty Stream

Whereas writing a book or creating a course on a website like Udemy.com is definitely not passive, the final product can produce a healthy passive income stream while potentially spawning various new opportunities through the contacts you will make.

If you decide to write a book, you will need to decide whether to pursue traditional publishing or self-publish. Both have their advantages. Traditional publishing comes with a great deal of structure and quality control. For self-published authors, the discipline to maintain quality control and stay on track timewise must come from within. On the plus side, you can receive much higher royalties as a self-published author.

Bitcoin and Cryptocurrency

In my humble opinion, even if a cryptocurrency does become widely established for a substantial timeframe, it will take luck for the "investor" to win in this space. The profusion of currencies will make it difficult to pick the winning horse. In closing, I will reference the profusion of ITOs[2] of the 17th century and leave it to you to decide whether cryptocurrency is "digital gold," as Robert Kiyosaki insists, or "pure FOMO," in the words of Warren Buffett.

"Dialing in" on the Proper Level of Passivity

Note that you can pursue these asset classes at varying levels of passivity. For example, if you want to enjoy passive income from triple net (NNN) lease retail, office, or industrial properties, you can directly own the real estate because once the purchase is made and the long-term lease is signed, you can enjoy the stream of passive income. On the other hand, if you want true passive

---

[2] Initial Tulip Offerings 🌷

income from apartments, you will definitely have to invest as a limited partner. Only you can decide the ideal level of passivity that suits your desires and your current stage of life. As you embark on your investment journey, consider your risk tolerance and desired level of involvement.

Cashflow is a Must! It is a good idea to invest a significant portion of your capital in cash-flowing (or liquid) investments. If you fail to do this, you may find yourself asset-rich but cash-poor. The following rhyme will help to keep you on track.

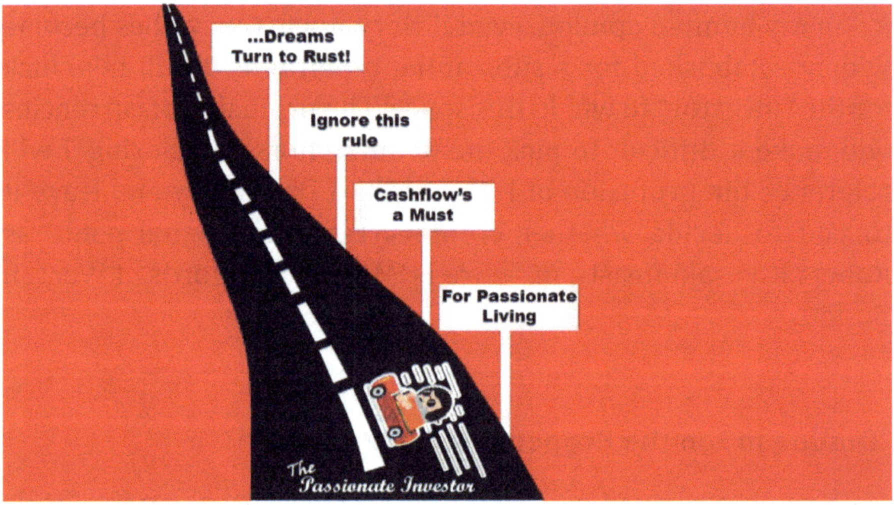

Summary of Asset Classes The table below summarizes the risks, expected returns, and other key features of alternative asset classes to help you digest this chapter's survey of the world of alternative asset classes.

Asset Class Comparison

	Stocks	Bonds	Real Estate Syndications	Private Equity	Private Lending	Early-Stage "Angel" / "Shark Tank"	Angel Fund
Nominal Returns	7%[1]	Variable	15% +[2]	11%[3]	12% +	27%[4]	27%[5]
Risks	Five S&P 500 drawdowns of 1/3 over the last 50 years	Negative real rate of return and duration.	Leverage can result in total loss of principal	Total loss	The need to foreclose to recover capital	Likely total loss	Illiquid, no control over portfolio composition
Benefits	High liquidity	High liquidity with low volatility	High returns	High and stable returns	High and stable returns	High returns	High returns
Drawbacks	High volatility	Likely long-term under-performance	Illiquid, but with cash flow	Illiquid	Illiquid, but with cash flow	Illiquid	Potential higher fees vs. individual investments
Time Horizon	Variable	Variable	5 Years	5 Years	Variable	7-10 Years	7-10 Years

[1] The S&P 500 has returned 7.15% between 2000 and 2023 assuming reinvestment of dividends. Source: https://www.officialdata.org/us/stocks/s-p-500/2000?amount=100&endYear=2023

[2] Scientific studies on real estate syndication returns are few and far between. Take the anecdotal 15% figure with a grain of salt considering that post-2008 returns have benefited from significant tailwinds.

[3] Returns between 2000 and 2023 according to CAIA Association. Source https://caia.org/blog/2024/04/23/long-term-private-equity-performance-2000-2023

[4] Studies of investment returns are performed on angel syndicates. Don't expect these returns if you "go it alone." Source: Robert Wiltbank, Willamette University, and Warren Boeker, University of Washington, 2007, Published by the Kauffman Foundation. URL: https://www.angelcapitalassociation.org/data/Documents/Resources/AngelGroupResarch/1d%20-%20Resources%20-%20Research/6%20RSCH_-_ACEF_-_Returns_to_Angel_Investor_in_Groups.pdf?rev=8AF0

[5] We can expect angel funds to produce similar returns to individual startup investments. The main difference is volatility. Caveat, you may pay more in fees for the convenience and diversification offered by the fund.

Online Resources from George's Award-Winning Real Estate and Private Markets Podcast: The Foundery–Where Leaders are Forged Daily!

Syndication with Pace Morby Episode

Retail and NNN

Nothing but Net (NNN) with Dan Lewkowicz

- Part I Part II

Living the (NNN) Dream Episode
with David Cruz-Palmer

Medical Office Investing Episode
with Ben Reinberg

Industrial RE with no Debt
with Joel Friedland Episode

Self-Storage Episode
with Taylor Loht

Senior Housing with Greg Bronson

- Part I   Part II

Private Lending Episode with Greg Bronson

Franchises Episode with Jon Ostenson

Now that we have taken a whirlwind tour of public and private markets, it is time for you to pick the asset classes you will invest in and begin the long process of becoming an expert in that asset class. In the next chapter, I will explore due diligence on investment opportunities.

Finding the Right Passive Income Opportunity

"The first rule is that you must not fool yourself, and you are the easiest one to fool."

Richard Feynman

The world of alternative assets can be an exciting (and also scary) place to explore. Let's face it, there is a reason that most people stick to stocks and bonds. It is so much easier to play it "safe," so to speak, by following the crowd. If you want to get ripped off year after year by mutual fund loads or investment advisor fees, go ahead. However, I suspect that if you have gotten this far, you may be after something more. The road ahead is difficult, and if you haven't traveled it before, it can seem treacherous. With a little effort, you will begin to spot the pitfalls. Although there is no substitute for experience, as they say, "the intelligent learn from their mistakes, the wise learn from the mistakes of others." You will need to rapidly become sophisticated to swim in these waters. So, let's dive in and start learning to swim!

The ideal investment combines three things: a great leadership team, a great deal, and your unique needs as an investor. We'll start with the leadership team.

The Leadership Team (Sponsor)

One of the many things that Warren Buffett looks for in a company is a high-quality management team that is strongly aligned with its shareholders. "Bet on the jockey, not the horse" is the constant refrain of successful investors. In a down market, a good operator can mean the difference between breaking even and making a solid return. It may even mean the difference between losing a property to foreclosure and being able to hold on until the good times return.

A good track record means more than having operated in the asset class before. Suppose you are investing in an apartment. There are huge differences between the operation of properties of classes A, B, and C. Unfortunately, the skills don't always translate well. Even the vendor contacts may not translate well. An experienced operator in a market will have solid property management contacts. But that doesn't mean that it would be a good idea for an operator to use the property management company from the last class C project on the next project if it is a freshly built class A property. Track record goes much deeper than property class.

Each business plan is unique. If the business plan includes, for example, Section 8 tenants or obtaining a HUD loan, and the lead operators lack experience in these areas, that may not necessarily be a "red flag," but it does indicate where the risk in the business plan is likely to emerge. The answer may be as simple as "Our property management company handles Section 8 tenants regularly," or "Jessica on the general partner team has a couple of properties with HUD loans."

Be sure to consider the complexity of the business plan as well. It is not enough to have a construction expert on the team. Even if the construction manager has run construction on the same asset class in the past, that may not be enough to guarantee successful execution. There is a huge gulf between a cosmetic renovation involving flooring and cabinets and a structural renovation that involves roofs, mechanicals, and changes to the

The Ideal Deal: A Three-Legged Stool Take away any of these three legs, and the ideal deal "stool" will not stand. Far too many new investors focus only on the deal.

floor plan. Has mold been discovered? That is an entirely different can of worms. Be sure that the construction team is up to the job.

Track record is not a silver bullet! What worked yesterday may not work in the future. Or even worse, yesterday's "hot idea" may be today's riskiest investment. Even bad investment theses can play out marvelously over a relatively short time frame. The most spectacular failures in financial history all share one thing in common – a great track record. If you still need convincing, just take a walk down memory lane with Long-Term Capital Management in the sidebar.

Long-Term Capital Management and the Limits of "Track Record"

Founded in 1994 by some of the greatest minds on Wall Street, Long-Term Capital Management (LTCM) was, in its time, the darling of Wall Street. The company made its money by executing a variety of trading strategies that involved the use of derivatives. With their founder John Merriweather, former head of bond trading at Salomon Brothers, at the helm and with Nobel Laureates Myron Scholes and Robert C. Merton, two of the developers of the Black-Scholes derivative pricing model, on the board, the company appeared unstoppable. And, for a time, they were. With outsized gains exceeding 40% in their early years, it seemed that this team could do nothing but win.

So, what exactly went wrong? Pride goeth before the fall, and so it went with LTCM. With so many wins under their belt, the leadership of the company became more and more complacent. Lacking a healthy fear of debt, they allowed themselves to become very heavily leveraged. Their over-confidence led them into concentrated trades. After all, if you have always been right, why diversify? The combination of concentration and leverage put LTCM in such a position that any financial turmoil could easily bring down their house of cards. In 1997 and 1998, twin crises would lead the company to their ruin. The Asian Financial Crisis of 1997 and the Russian Economic Crisis of 1998 were the one-two punch that led to a $3.6 billion bailout and subsequent dissolution of the company in early 2000.

In the final analysis, a track record is always highly desirable. However, never rely too heavily on the track record when making an investment. Ask yourself, "What happens when the world changes?". Because the world will change and change again before you retire, and if your investment thesis can be washed out by a watershed economic event, it probably will be. Be wary of leverage, and no matter how certain you are in your investment thesis - diversify!

Communication

Effective communication isn't just a pre-investment consideration; it's the lifeline of your investment journey. Clear, ongoing communication can mitigate risks and enhance your overall experience. A good operator will communicate with you often. Most importantly, a good communicator will be forthright about what is going wrong. If you are unhappy with the quality of communication before you wire your funds, consider this a red flag - you are unlikely to find the communication more to your liking after you wire. In any event, you should never move forward with anything that you aren't comfortable with.

There are many things that you will want to ask your sponsor including asking for references. Particularly because alternative assets are a small world, most people won't say anything negative, so you may have to dig a bit. You can ask about hurdles that the project faced, and how the sponsor dealt with them. You can also ask whether these setbacks communicated clearly and forthrightly. The classic "Would you invest with this sponsor again?" is also a great way to let people express a degree of reservation even if they are unwilling to say something negative outright.

The Deal

This is the obvious part, and unfortunately, for most investors, this is the only element of the offering that they consider. When you vet a deal, you need to carefully consider the margin of safety that the deal provides. Are rents below market? Does the deal cash flow from day one? Does the deal involve fixed debt or a rate cap? Are there multiple exit strategies? Is the company properly capitalized (working capital, capital expenditures, contingencies, etc.)? Do the partners have deep enough pockets to avoid a capital call if things go sideways? It is the margin of safety that protects not only your desired return but your principal as well. Living to fight another day is paramount.

Return Metrics

To make sense of the documents that you will need to peruse before investing in a private equity transaction, we will discuss some financial terminology to make things easier. Most often, returns are expressed in terms of internal rate of return (IRR). Technically speaking, this is the discount rate that sets the present value of all cash flows to zero. More intuitively, you can think of IRR as a measure of return that takes into account the timing of cash flows. Since you can reinvest your distributions, taking timing into account is a strength of this method. However, IRR also assumes that you will be able to reinvest your distributions at the same rate of return. This "reinvestment risk" will cause your actual rate of return to diverge from the calculated IRR if you end up reinvesting your distributions at a lower rate of return.

Another way to express returns is to simply divide the total cash returned by the total cash invested. In real estate, this is generally referred to as the equity multiple or "equity mult." In more traditional private equity, this is often referred to as "multiple on invested capital" or MOIC (pronounced "moyk").

Cash on cash (CoC) return expresses the percentage of total invested cash that is returned through operations during the holding period. Be on the lookout for operators who falsely include the cash from disposition or refinance as "cash flow." This is a red flag that the operator is unsophisticated. A cash-out refinance can, however, increase your CoC by reducing the cash invested going forward.

Underwriting / Modeling Returns

The key to understanding any deal is digging into the underwriting. Most slide decks will just show you a snapshot of the cash flow and projected returns. This is not enough! You should receive the original underwriting from the sponsor upon request. Make a point of not only requesting the underwriting but also make a point of re-underwriting the deal yourself. There are many free or cheap underwriting tools available. Even if you end up paying for your underwriting tool, the money you spend is a drop in the bucket compared to what you may lose in the event of a deal that goes sideways or which even fails to meet expected returns. If you can prevent even one lackluster investment by underwriting every deal you invest in, it will be worth it.

Everyone should be an underwriter. It is the only way you can protect yourself in a sea of sharks. The world is full of investors who fooled themselves into thinking they found a money-printing machine. Never fall in love with your investments! They are inanimate objects. It may sound crazy, but it happens.

Underwriting is so much more than just putting numbers in a spreadsheet. Underwriting begins when you understand the certainty and provenance of every number in the spreadsheet. I will consider real estate underwriting here. How strong are your rent projections? Did you pull your own comps or at least dive into the comps provided? What about the insurance? Do you have at least a soft quote? Depending on how far along the deal is, you may (or should) already have a hard quote for insurance. When is the next tax assessment? Does the tax assessment take into account the purchase price? What percentage of the purchase price is generally assessable in your locality (this is something that you may be able to find through a reputable broker or through the knowledge of a trusted operator from that market)? Some large projects even engage a tax consultant to estimate the new taxes.

The most difficult issue in modeling a deal is the fact that no two deals are alike. When you underwrite an investment, make sure that you are using a purpose-built spreadsheet tool to underwrite the deal. Don't get comfortable with multifamily, and then use your multifamily tool to underwrite a mobile home park, or vice-versa. That's like trying to pound a square peg into a round hole. To find free models appropriate for dozens of situations, check out Adventures in CRE at https://www.adventuresincre.com/.

If you are purchasing an operating business, ensure that you are comfortable with reading the financial statements. You also need to be able to assess what the seller may be hiding and whether you trust the numbers on the page. If you can't get ahold of tax returns and bank statements, you may need to spend time alongside the owner to ensure that the business is producing the projected returns. The level of due diligence required to purchase an operating business goes far beyond the scope of this book. Those who are in the game to buy an operating business have probably been corporate leaders in the past or started a business. If that doesn't sound like you (yet), don't despair. There are many things that you can do to build yourself up to that level, including learning financial accounting through financial statement analysis as an equities investor and starting that first business! Passive investing is a journey, not a destination.

Modeling returns is only the first step in the process. You will need to ensure that you are happy with the market. For a real estate deal, this would include a solid understanding of the current general health of that asset class at this time and in the near to medium term. In addition, you will want to assess the growth prospects of the city, and the neighborhood and adjoining neighborhoods as well. A great (and free) guide to performing these analyses is provided by Neal Bawa's free 40-minute "Realfocus" course currently available at Udemy. For an operating business, you would want to focus on the size of the market, major competitors, and barriers to entry.

Generally, most of the cash flows will come upon disposition. The sales price will depend on the cap rate at the time of sale, meaning that your assumptions regarding the exit cap rate will greatly influence your predicted returns. You will want to perform a sensitivity analysis to ensure that you may expect solid returns across various exit cap rates.

Look at the IRR on That One!

The slide deck is designed to dazzle you. Just as a 10-K (annual report) from a publicly traded company is full of glossy pictures and exciting financial projections that are "up and to the left," the slide deck is full of pretty, shiny objects. The real news in the annual report is buried in the back. This is where you find the financial statements and the footnotes that provide clues as to how to interpret those statements. Unfortunately, for investors in private markets, you need to dig deep into the underwriting to get the full answers to your questions.

The biggest mistake that new investors make is to simply look at the exciting projections of returns and use these to decide where to invest. Sponsors differ widely with respect to how "conservative" their underwriting is, and projects differ widely in terms of the number of hurdles and the difficulty in surmounting them. When you re-underwrite the deal, you should consider not only the IRR estimate that you believe to be most realistic but also the likelihood of the realistic scenario versus the optimistic and the downside scenarios as well.

Consider the two investments in the table below with vastly different expected returns. Investment A has the highest estimated likelihood of returning 15% and virtually no likelihood of total loss. Investment B is most likely to return 25% per annum, but there is also a 20% likelihood of total loss. Perhaps surprisingly, the two investments would have the exact same outcome after five years, namely a 2.14 equity multiple. If it were my money, I would select investment A and sleep better at night.

Two Very Different Investments? The two investments described in this table have very different expected return distributions but...exactly the same projected five-year equity multiple. One will have you sleep better at night.

	Likelihood of Scenario		5 - year
Scenario	Investment A	Investment B	Equity Multiple
Total Loss	0%	20%	0
5% IRR	10%	5%	1.28
15% IRR	70%	20%	2.01
25% IRR	20%	55%	3.05
Equity Multiple	2.14	2.14	

You

It may seem that after all the vetting above, we should be good to go, right? Well, no. An investment might promise high returns, but if it doesn't align with your liquidity needs or risk tolerance, it may not be the best fit for your portfolio. An investment in an early-stage company that returns 10x in seven years may be great from an investment returns standpoint, but if you suffer a medical emergency and have to send your children to college in the meantime, you may feel extraordinarily crunched for money in the meantime.

Suppose that you have no need for cash flow because you are already "set." You may decide to invest only in deals that reasonably project the highest internal rate of return (IRR). Additionally, you may be investing through your self-directed IRA, which won't even allow you to enjoy the benefits of cash flow in the present (we'll talk more about the benefits of a self-directed IRA and how to get yourself set up in a later chapter). Deals that provide cash flow can still hold significant advantages for these types of investors as well. Cash flow can provide a sizeable margin of safety which can substantially increase your actual returns over time, and it is only your actual returns over time that you will collect. Above all, never rely on projected returns! Do your own due diligence.

Your Investment Thesis

To know whether something "fits" your goals, you need to rigorously define how you plan to reach your goals through a formal investment thesis. To do this properly, you need to concisely define what you are investing in and why. You will also need to consider the timing of expected cash flows and how this timing fits in with your goals.

Fleshing out your ideas and your assumptions will help to frame the lessons you learn through investing. Writing your thesis down is the best way to do this. The clarity that comes with writing will benefit you both through streamlining your decision-making process, as well as in helping you to create your "brand" as an investor. Being able to concisely define your "buy box" will make you easy to work with. Nobody wants to waste time sending deals to someone who is not interested. On the other hand, if your buy box is clearly defined, you will find yourself at the top of the list when suitable deals come along.

Certain asset classes, like redevelopment, come with more surprises than newer stabilized properties. You should always ask yourself the question, "Will I sleep well at night?". If not, even if the expected returns materialize, the investment isn't going to be worth the agony.

Take your time to find the right opportunity. You don't have to "swing at every pitch." Warren Buffett is known for maintaining his stock of "dry powder," which he keeps in cash and Treasuries (yes, you heard that correctly).

Pillar II: Take Immediate and Massive Action

Woohoo! Now that we have leveled up our knowledge required to uncover hidden opportunities, we are ready to begin the second major leg of our journey – "Take Immediate and Massive Action." Take a deep breath. We are about to begin to implement the practices that will provide you with the passive income that will provide you with the freedom to live the life you deserve.

Without action, knowledge is useless. However, we are after a quality of action befitting a life of passion. We aren't going to focus solely on the execution of building passive income, we are going to work on living a life of passion and excitement along the way. The terrain gets a bit steeper from here, but I guarantee that the view is worth it.

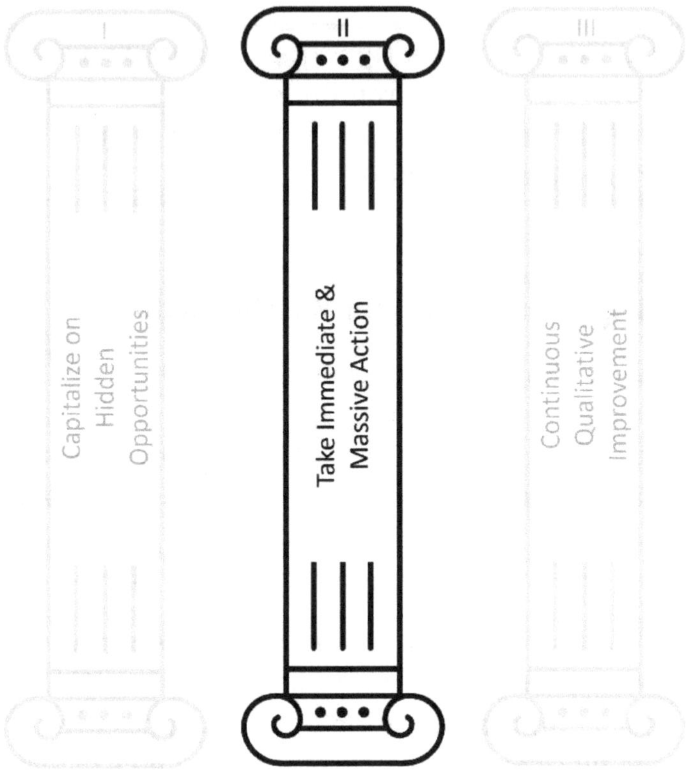
I
Capitalize on Hidden Opportunities
II
Take Immediate & Massive Action
III
Continuous Qualitative Improvement

The Truth About Passive Investing: It's Not as Easy as It Seems!

"You know it don't come easy..."

Ringo Starr

If you have made it this far, I hope the following sentence doesn't shock you. (Psst)...passive investing is still work! The "passive" part only comes after you sign the legal documents and wire your money (more on the mechanics of passive investing below). To be a great passive investor, you will have to do a lot of the same things that active investors do. The difference is that you can spend *most* of your time doing whatever you want.

This chapter will focus on the following six things that every great passive investor must know:

1. The mechanics of making passive investments
2. Vetting the opportunity
3. Monitoring the operations (learning and growing)
4. Learning from mistakes (the *great* investor's feedback loop)
5. Networking and growing (widening the funnel)
6. Never stop learning (return to step 2 as a humble seeker, collect $200 cash flow)

The Mechanics of Passive Investing

Investing in private placements like private equity or real estate syndications involves several milestones:

Contacting a Sponsor

With the exception of stocks and bonds, most of the opportunities described herein will require that you become acquainted with deal sponsors that manage the asset for the benefit of the owners. You can start by searching for "apartment syndication" or some similar search term.

Like so many things in life, it is a bit of a numbers game. Ideally, you should read as many books and watch as many YouTube videos as you can to cast the widest net possible. That doesn't mean that you should necessarily go with the sponsor that has the greatest number of "views" or "likes" or the sponsor that has the best-selling title. It has been said, "The loudest voice in the room isn't necessarily the one you should be listening to." Working through someone local, particularly someone that you already know and trust, can have its advantages as well. You will definitely want to have access to your sponsor. Someone local may be significantly more accessible, which is particularly important if you are newer to the game.

Sophisticated or Accredited

Your sponsor will need to get to know you a little bit before you can proceed to passive income nirvana. The sponsor will need to determine that you are a sophisticated investor, generally through a video conference and a questionnaire. Essentially, this means that you have the ability to fully understand the risks involved in the investment you are making.

Accredited status broadens your investment opportunities significantly, requiring verification through financial statements or CPA letters. This means that you have a net worth of $1 million, not including your primary residence, or that you make $200K per year, or that you and your spouse combined make $300K per year. Holders of certain financial accreditations, including Series

7, Series 65, or Series 82, are also accredited investors. Most syndications and all private equity or angel investments will require you to be accredited unless you are investing through a crowdfunding platform.

Vetting the Investment

Vetting your opportunity is the essence of passive investing and involves far more than we can discuss in this section. Accordingly, I have devoted the entire chapter entitled "Finding the Right Passive Opportunity" to this topic. Since passive opportunities are as diverse as the businesses they are based upon, you will find additional tips on vetting investments in the chapter entitled "Passive Income - A World of Opportunity" under the section relating to each of the various types of passive investments. To simplify matters, we will focus on real estate syndications in this chapter. Although details will differ, other types of investments will utilize the same or similar documents.

Triage, Always Triage!

Making proper passive investments is work, a lot of work. You simply can't do the required work on each opportunity that comes your way. There are simply too many opportunities available for you to carefully consider each of them. Just as a battlefield doctor must sadly ignore the most heavily wounded, you must triage your investment opportunities. Most of them won't fit your desired risk or return profile. They may come from sponsors who you simply don't know enough about to make a proper determination of trust, or you may simply not like the market. The better you know your investment criteria, the better you can triage the opportunities that simply don't fit, and, thus, the more energy you will have to properly focus on the opportunities that do fit your basic criteria. Doing the appropriate level of due diligence and triage go hand in hand.

Putting your investment thesis in writing is a great way to simplify the process of triage. There is nothing like writing out your ideas to bring clarity to your thinking. By writing (and rewriting) your thesis, you will be able to rapidly rule out investments that don't meet your investment goals.

Legal Due Diligence

Understanding legal documents is paramount. You can always consult a lawyer with any questions you have regarding the legal documentation involved in any private placement. That doesn't mean that you can afford to not personally understand what goes into the legal documents you will be signing. Without a solid understanding of what the legal documents mean, how will you know what questions to ask? Your lawyer is skilled at interpreting the law. When it comes to reading minds, not so much.

Private Placement Memorandum

Part of the work of vetting an investment involves reading the legal documents. Of all the documents you will receive, the private placement memorandum (PPM) can be the most intimidating, although it shouldn't be. The PPM is full of every reason that you *shouldn't* invest in this opportunity. It will detail everything that can go wrong. It is written in such a way as to suggest that you are crazy if you invest in this offering.

Now, if you are wondering why I say that it shouldn't be intimidating, it is because this shouldn't be the first time you have read a document like this. If you invest in equities, you should be reading forms 10-K and 10-Q for the companies you invest in, better known as your friendly annual and quarterly reports. These documents are also written by lawyers to dot every "i" and cross every "t" by reminding you of every way that the company could lose money. It can be valuable to read this section very carefully, particularly the first time you make an investment in a new asset class to ensure that you are completely familiar with the risks involved.

You will often find a "summary of investment" section that includes a description of the company and the asset being invested in. This section will tell you many things about the securities offered. It will also generally remind you that the securities are illiquid and may not be resold and that you will have to fill out a subscription agreement, and that there will also be a questionnaire to determine your suitability as an investor. If there are multiple classes of shares, their characteristics may be summarized here as well along with a brief biography of the general partners.

Operating Agreement (OA)

This document formally specifies how the legal entity you are forming is to be run. Let's use real estate as an example to keep it simple. All partners (both general partners and limited partners) will sign an OA for the company that will own the building that you are purchasing. This OA will state that this LLC is "manager-managed" and will specify the name of the "manager," which will be another LLC. This second LLC will have the general partners as members. This "dual layer" structure separates the decision-making entity (the "manager") from the limited partners in the manager-managed LLC.

Risk Factors

This is the longest section of the PPM and contains every potential risk that a team of distinctly risk-averse attorneys was able to devise. The risks vary from the more or less obvious (interest rates may rise, inflation may damage the value of the capital returned, and that the real estate market may become less seller-friendly before the disposition of the property or that the premises could be damaged in a flood) to the unlikely (an act of terrorism could result in uninsured losses) to the fact that you might not get your K-1 on time resulting in your tax preparer having to file an extension which is sadly a near certainty. The value in reading through the entire PPM is in ensuring that you do, in fact, understand all of the risks involved in making the investment.

Reading the PPM carefully will help you understand how the passive investing rule works. Consider the following nugget of wisdom straight from an actual PPM on side letters: "The Manager may enter into 'Side Letter' (also known as 'sidecar') agreements with one or more investors in which the Manager grants said investors specific rights benefits or privileges...". If you are contributing a significant portion of the capital for the project, you may ask for and receive such benefits. With most syndications advertising minimums of around $50K, if you are contributing significantly more than this, you should inquire as to whether you can obtain concessions such as an additional 1% preferred return. If you are contributing $200K or more, you may want to ask for an additional 2% preferred return. Many large syndications will already have multiple shareholder classes with corresponding tiered returns. However, the sponsors of a smaller syndication may not have provided for the unlikely event that one investor will provide a large proportion of the capital required for the project. "Ask and ye shall receive..." You have nothing to lose by trying.

Subscription Agreement

This document details the "nuts and bolts" of your investment purchase. This is where you will indicate the number of shares you are purchasing and the price. If there are multiple classes of shares, this is where you will indicate the class of shares that you are buying. In many cases, all the above documents will be "rolled into one" for the sake of simplicity.

Monitoring the operations (learning and growing)

Being a passive investor is a great way to learn. Because being good at anything requires "staying in your lane," it is simply impossible for one person to be an active operator of a well-diversified portfolio. Since it is much easier to vet an investment than it is to find, close on, and then operate an investment, you can certainly invest in a wider range of investments as a passive investor. As an active investor, I always like to invest passively first in new asset classes to expand my knowledge, contacts, and experience before I consider operating that asset class myself.

Learning From Mistakes (the *great* investor's feedback loop)

It is a good idea to compile a list of lessons learned from each investment, *regardless of the outcome*. It's an even better idea when an investment fails to provide its expected return or loses money. A good way to start down this path is to keep the story of each investment in a Word file or similar. The first thing this file should include is your rationale for investing. It need not be long. Think of it as a narrative. Include only the most relevant facts. You don't need to include the supporting evidence, this should be in the supporting docs such as the OM, underwriting, sales and rent comps, and other research that you and the general partners did on the deal.

Your story of the investment should also include the various twists and turns along the way and what you learned. Doing a full post-mortem on all of the investments in your portfolio, from stocks to real estate and beyond, will help you identify your weaknesses and blind spots as an investor. This is how you steepen the learning curve. Charlie Munger is an example of a great investor who lives by the rule of learning from each investment mistake.

Learning From the Mistakes of Others (Expert Level)

Now, how do you take this common-sense advice up a notch or three? It has been said that the intelligent learn from their own mistakes, but the wise learn from the mistakes of others. If you don't want to have to learn everything the hard way, you need to find a way to leverage a wider network. Talking to other people can expose you to a much wider array of deals than you could ever come into contact with on your own.

A podcast is a great way for me to leverage a network of highly successful investors. I make a point of diving deep each week and asking questions such as "Describe a mistake or misstep and how it set you up for future success" or "Name one mistake that you see among operators in your field." The tips and tricks I get from these sources are invaluable! Considering the time and expense involved in setting up your own podcast, I am not suggesting that you go this route unless you are already inclined to do so. If you do decide to "give it a whirl," there is no shortage of resources to get you started.

Mentoring and masterminds provide another source of exposure to deals. As an active investor, mentoring newer investors is one of my key sources of deal flow. If you want access to the wisdom of the community in a less time-intensive manner, find a group of passive investors who are at a similar point in their journey and meet weekly via videoconference.

Networking and Growing (Widening the Funnel)

When it comes to learning and growing, meeting other investors is the "thin edge of the wedge." Conferences can be a great way to meet investors. If you want to grow your network on a budget, you can try virtual conferences or videoconference networking calls. If you are looking for a place to start, may I humbly suggest "CRE Network at Noon Eastern" where you can meet dozens of great investors as well as yours truly, the host of the show each Wednesday!

Never stop learning (return to step 2 as a humble seeker, collect $200 cash flow)

Always remember that "Pride preceedeth the fall." The worst thing any investor can do is to begin to think that they "know." It is always safer to operate as a seeker of ever-changing reality. What worked yesterday may be a prescription for disaster tomorrow. No asset class, market or operating strategy remains the best approach for long. The world will change and change again before you reach passionate living bliss.

On the other hand, if you learn and grow every day, nothing can stop you. Many an investor has overcome an early stumble or even bankruptcy through determination. Even if you must "start over," you will be starting at a much higher level if you do a full post-mortem on all your mistakes, both large and small. It may help to think of change not as a criticism of the past, but as a sign of growth.

Syndication Revisited

Most investors tend to "pick a horse" and then run with it for far too long before reevaluating whether that is the ideal investment vehicle to continue to ride into the future. Let's consider syndication as an example.

Syndication is an investment vehicle that has grown significantly, particularly over the years since the Great Recession. One reason for the high returns that have been produced by real estate syndication is the housing crisis we find ourselves in. If you asked me, "Is real estate syndication a good place to invest?", my answer is "Yes, and for the foreseeable future," because the housing crisis isn't going away any time soon because our anemic construction industry will take a long time to grow strong enough to bridge the gap.

However, a true investor never "falls in love" with any asset class. Unlike the "true love" you feel for a perfect lover, as an investor, you must love conditionally and always be ready to change when the facts change. No trend continues unabated indefinitely. Your asset allocation mix must change accordingly. You must focus on a subset of the investment world to be good at what you do. But which subset of the potential investment universe you are focusing on should always be gradually changing.

To consider just how long a(n exceptional) trend may continue, let's look at how Apple stock has done since its IPO. After adjusting for splits, one share of AAPL stock would have cost ten cents when it became a publicly traded company on December 12, 1980. Over the next 43.5 years, the share price grew over 1940 times its initial value representing a compound annual growth rate of 19%[3]. If that sounds amazing, consider that angel investor and employee number three, Mike Markkula, made over 100 times his original money on his initial investment up to the IPO just under four years later. That represents a rate of return of over 200% per annum!

In summary, although the likelihood of any positive trend continuing as long as Apple Inc. is vanishingly small. The moral of the story is that unless you believe that you lead a truly charmed life, you will almost certainly have to change horses from time to time. Be sure to "do your homework" on asset classes and don't just stick with what is familiar to you.

---

[3] Calculated as of June 4, 2024. Including (the paltry) dividends increases the total return from 19.02% to 19.05%.

Building Your Active Lifestyle One Brick at a Time

"How do you eat an elephant? One bite at a time."

- Unknown

Building an active lifestyle and accumulating wealth can feel overwhelming, but like eating an elephant, it's accomplished one bite at a time. This chapter uses the metaphor of 'bricks' to guide you through constructing a more passionate and active life, one step at a time. These 'bricks' are structured progressively so that you can start racking up quick wins today while you continue to work on the bigger goals.

These successes that you experience from following this plan will be the mortar that keeps these bricks in place, so it is important that you stop reading at the end of each section to complete the task. This will help you integrate these practices into your life and will make the positive changes permanent. Creating a success of any size, if it is meaningful to you will set a positive tone. People give up because they don't feel the win - feel the win today!

Above all, remember to take action, but don't get overwhelmed. Making major changes in life is hard, somewhat like catching a bowling ball. If I toss you two bowling balls at the same time, you will probably drop both. We are planning this in a stepwise fashion so that we can catch those bowling balls, but one at a time, I promise.

Active income is still part of the equation for all but my lucky few retired readers out there. As such, we need to address the "work" aspect of your life. This chapter will take a broader perspective. We are going to start to widen the circle of focus from investing to work and finally to personal life so that we can make the greatest possible impact.

Let's start laying the bricks for an even more passionate existence!

Brick 1 – Schedule Your High-Impact Tasks

Scheduling time for your most important tasks ensures that urgent but less important activities don't dominate your day. Identify (and calendar) the top tasks that will "move the needle" in your business or investing career each day. These should be "vision" items that change the course of your business, not the "housekeeping" tasks that simply need to get done throughout the course of the day. Dedicate morning hours, when you're most focused, to these high-impact tasks to maximize productivity."

All day long, I have calendar reminders popping up to remind me to write this book or some similar game-changing task like planning out the next season of my real estate and passive income podcast "The Foundery – Where Leaders are Forged Daily." If you make a discipline of continually identifying and blocking out time for the tasks that truly move the needle, you will feel a significant "productivity dividend" in no time. Make sure that you don't just plow all the time you just freed up through greater productivity back into the business. It is important to ensure that you put a significant portion of this time into yourself and your relationships so that your gains become self-sustaining.

Realize that every minute you are working on high-impact tasks, you are earning your passive income enterprise money and reducing the quality of your life experience. On the other hand, every minute you are working on lower-level tasks, you are *costing* yourself money.

Task (mortar): Define your top tasks that "move the needle" in your business or investments. Choose no more than three tasks and schedule a block between one and three hours each weekday to work on these tasks. My recurring calendar subject heading looks like this: "Top Tasks Until 11 AM: Writing & Deal Vetting." From time to time, I update with up to three tasks. Whenever possible, put the tasks that move the needle in the morning when you are sharpest and have the fewest distractions. Keeping on track with your high-impact tasks will help you grow your productivity significantly which will help you have the flexibility to stop when a reminder to enjoy one of your preferred activities pops up (see Brick 2 below). Remember to work on the business, not in the business. As for the less demanding tasks like laundry, you can always do these later in the day when your energy and focus are lagging.

So, does calendaring work? You are reading this book, aren't you? Calendar reminders helped me stay on track. Now, let it work for you!

Brick 2 - Schedule your Passion(s)!

You should also calendar time for activities you're passionate about. Scheduling these activities ensures they become a priority. Even if work occasionally interrupts, knowing you have these moments planned will help you stay motivated and manage your time better. Every important recurring task like "have a late after-school lunch with the kids" or "buffer time to drive to Argentine tango lesson" is on my calendar. I even schedule reminders to take time to enjoy literature because I know that it deepens my existence, but I won't do it if I am not reminded.

Of course, there are times when I can't drop everything to execute the task described in the time block on the calendar. There will be times that I am working under the pressure of a deadline or on a crucial task. There is nothing wrong with ignoring the calendar reminder under these circumstances. If you start noticing a pattern, it is time to ask some questions.

It is important to schedule at least some time for one of your passions each evening, even if it is just 15 minutes. Knowing that you will spend time doing something that you love later today will make you work more efficiently. Choosing not to answer a time-wasting email (or responding extra tersely) is much easier when you know that your 15 minutes of passion time can easily become 30 (or zero) depending on how well or poorly you manage your time throughout the day.

As a personal example, I use the "carrot" of playing guitar in the evenings to sharpen my discipline for avoiding time-wasting tasks. When I see that (e.g. useless news article link), I think about my guitar collection and how many days I didn't save at least five minutes to play. I consciously commit to five to fifteen guilt-free minutes with my guitar by telling myself that I just freed up at least that much time by avoiding something fruitless. Try this out for yourself and watch your productive time "multiply."

Task (mortar): Pick a single thing that you would love to do (or would love to do more of) and calendar this too. When you find your concentration flagging during the day, remind yourself that this fun calendar reminder will fire later today and that if you get back on track now, you won't be forced to ignore it. When it comes to the "fun task," don't overthink it. This method is about improvisation, we aren't committing to any particular act or discipline. We are committing to a process of discovery, a process of spontaneity in discipline, not unlike Alan Watts' description of Zen.

Most importantly, don't overthink it. If you think of a more suitable task later, don't worry, you can change it. What is most important is that you choose something so that you can have your first win before life distracts you from your goal.

Brick 3 - Set Boundaries

Identify tasks that drain your energy and delegate them. For example, outsource bookkeeping or data analysis to free up your time for more impactful work. Additionally, establish boundaries by setting aside days free from meetings. I've reserved Fridays for personal growth and family time, which has greatly improved my work-life balance.

Along the way, you will encounter various mental blocks that you will need to overcome. When it comes to bookkeeping, many small business owners are afraid to let go of this task because they are concerned about information security. You can grant read-only redacted access to your bank account to a bookkeeper or provide redacted statements.

If bookkeeping is not the issue, I guarantee that there is at least one investment or business task that you can farm out. Need data analysis for your investments? If you can "sanitize" the raw data of anything sensitive, you can send it to someone overseas who can free up much-needed time. You should have already put a value on your time in the last chapter. Now it is time to use that value. Anything that can be done for less than that price is ripe for farming out.

Another great way to create boundaries is to block off an entire day from meetings. I have blocked off my Fridays for over two years for family and personal growth. The benefits are tremendous. Not only does this make the stressful schedule-driven part of the week shorter, but it also means I can take the fam on a three-day weekend at the drop of a hat! When the need to schedule an important meeting arises, I always have Friday as a fallback. Whether you are using the calendar to set small boundaries like I did in Brick 1 for an after-school lunch with the kids, or larger boundaries, like Fridays off, this is one technique that can have you experiencing wins from day one!

Brick 4 – Join Forces with Your Spouse

With newfound efficiency and time, involve your spouse in your journey. Share how these changes have positively impacted you and discuss ways to support each other's dreams. This collaborative approach can strengthen your relationship and help you achieve common goals.

Though it may seem strange, this approach of "work smarter, live larger" doesn't come naturally to everyone. If you are having trouble getting your spouse to join you on this journey, you need some WIFFMs, as in, "What's in it for me?" You can highlight the ways in which these approaches have made you a better spouse, parent, or lover. You can also suggest ways in which a lifestyle of passive income will help your lover live out their dreams. If that doesn't work, suggesting a spa day never fails.

Task (mortar): Have a goal-setting chat with your significant other tonight if you haven't already. You can start by sharing this book. If your significant other is not much of a bookworm, try summarizing one insight or breakthrough from your reading each night.

Brick 5 – Goal Check

Time to get back to that "productivity dividend"! I am expecting that by "Brick 5," you have built a significant amount of "margin" in your life. Now, let's set some goals. Unlike the calendar reminders we set above, these goals should be for something deeper; they should be aspirations that make you proud. Each week, set three goals and schedule time to work on them. Keeping these goals visible and top-of-mind will ensure you stay on track. Calendar reminders can be very versatile!

A great way to do this is to take a moment to briefly celebrate three wins from last week. Next, review last week's goals. Did you accomplish these goals? More importantly, by engaging in the struggle, did you become a bigger person, the sort of person who can accomplish that goal? What did you do that made it possible to accomplish your goals this week? If something got in the way, how could you have dealt with this hurdle more productively?

Task (mortar): Now is the time to ensure that you are spending time most effectively by setting three goals for the week and putting them on your calendar for next Monday morning. Put them on a sticky note or some other visible place to keep them top-of-mind. Every time you see that sticky note, know that the reckoning is approaching rapidly! When you are tempted to ignore the reminder, ask yourself how you are going to feel on Monday morning when your calendar reminder pops up. Choose the actions that will make you proud!

Brick 6 – Hire Help; Success is Not a Solo Journey!

Consider hiring help in both your professional and personal life (virtual assistant, freelancer, or housekeeper). If you are cost-conscious, remind yourself that you are investing the time freed up for more financially impactful tasks. The beauty of this brick is that it is the gift that keeps giving. The more you use this tip, the more you have the scope to use it further.

All entrepreneurs say that they are "doing it for their family." But how many entrepreneurs actually take the time to ask their families what they want? By giving a gift that frees up your loved one's time through childcare, tutoring, or housework, you are providing the space for your spouse to invest directly in themselves. An investment in yourself pays dividends. An investment in your spouse is like compound interest.

Task (mortar): Consider hiring that VA, freelancer, housecleaner, or other professional today! You can thank me later!

Before we move on to more philosophical topics, I want to leave you with one final concrete idea. The ideal investment opportunity is found at the confluence of a strong leadership team, your goals, and strong particulars relating to the deal itself.

Pillar III - Continuous Qualitative Improvement

In Pillar I, we considered where to find hidden opportunities and how to approach them productively. In Pillar II, we began the crucial work of implementation by taking immediate and massive action. We are about to embark on the final and most important leg of our journey, where we focus on continuous, qualitative improvement.

If you are still unsure of how you are going to reach your lofty goals, fear not! Through a commitment to continuous improvement, your capacity to seize your dream life will grow by the day. If you are frustrated that your journey to success has not been a linear path, take heart in the fact that it never was for anyone in the history of this human race! Once you embrace that a true commitment to success is a commitment to starting over one thousand times with the scars and knowledge of the last stage of your journey, you are truly ready to embark. Pillar III unquestionably constitutes the most demanding part of the journey.

Remember, I told you that this is not a "get rich quick" book. *If* you are willing to get into the arena and are unafraid to have your face marred by "dust and sweat and blood.[4]" *then* I believe that *you will reach your goal*. You *will* arrive at your destination if you simply resolve not to give up. To paraphrase and repurpose the famous poem by Devon Brough: "Struggling

[4] Theodore Roosevelt "The Man in the Arena."

financially is hard, taking the steps to become financially independent is hard, choose your hard. Pick wisely"

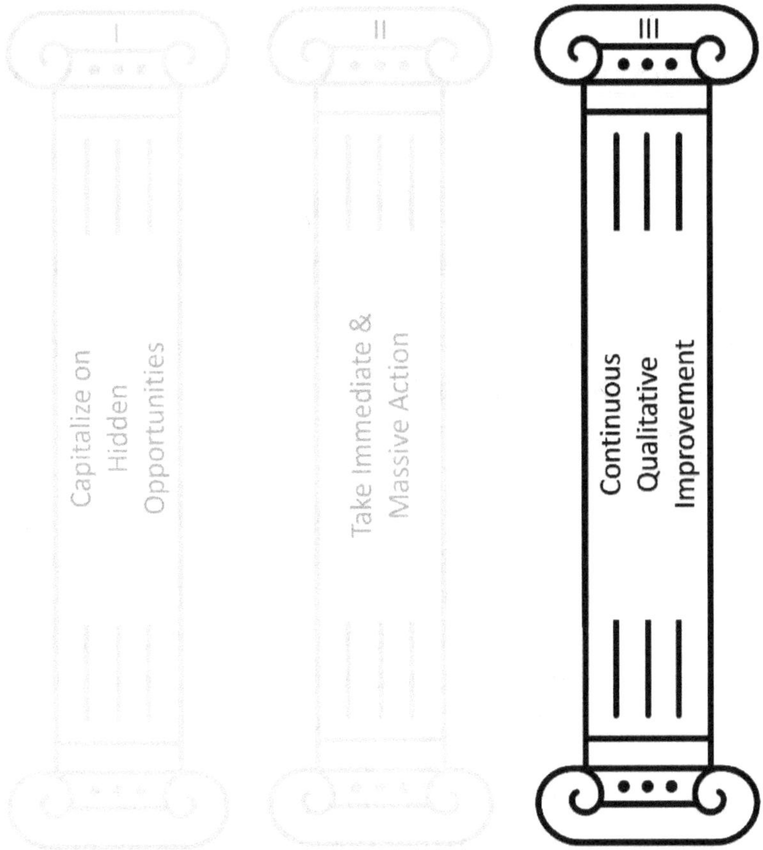

The Zen of Passive Investing: Mindfully Pursuing Wealth

"In Zen, there is no contradiction between... discipline in spontaneity and spontaneity in discipline."

- Alan W. Watts

Unlike almost every other book in the world that claims to teach you the Zen of something but ends up teaching you very little about that thing (and even less about Zen), In this chapter, I will delve deeply into the essence of both realms to uncover their mutual lessons. Are you ready? Let's go!

The Passive vs. Active Duality

Opposites feed each other. The ancient Chinese knew this in the 3rd century BC, and they codified this knowledge in the instantly recognizable yin-yang. As you see, contained within the yin (black), you will find a white dot and within the yang (white), a black dot. And so, everything contains a seed of its opposite. Though originating from Daoism, the yin-yang is also an element of Confucianism and Buddhism, which I will focus on here.

Ideally, we should practice active investing to become a better passive investor...and we practice passive investing to become a better active investor. As a passive investor, we know how we would like to be communicated with. As active investors, we should observe the golden rule regarding our passive investors (not the rule about "Whosoever has the gold...rules," I mean the other one, the one you learned as a child).

The Teacup Kōan

A professor came to study Zen with the Japanese master Nan-in. Before the formal lesson began (or so the guest believed), Nan-in served his guest a generous cup of tea. So generous in fact that the cup, now overflowing, began to spill onto the ground. The professor, no longer able to restrain himself exclaimed "But, the cup can hold no more, it is overfull".

"Like this cup," said Nan-in, "you are full of your own opinions. How can I show you Zen unless you first empty your cup?".

The full cup is tempting, but it is the empty cup we must seek. Like the professor, we must empty our cup of yesterday's stale investment advice to be receptive to new ideas and ways of thinking that will help us navigate the ever-changing investment landscape.

Likewise, as active investors, we learn how deals work inside and out. This knowledge must be built one way or another, so if you plan on being a passive investor, you will need to work that much harder to build it. Rather than trying to force the world into a "black" / "white" or "good" / "evil" dualism that doesn't always fit, Zen embraces the idea that the world is never precisely one thing or another. Here, opposites are not seen as antagonists but rather as night feeds into day and day into night, as cooperative and coequal. Our concepts are (or at least they can be) distracting overlays that we add to our experiences, and which cloud our ability to clearly perceive the intrinsic nature of reality.

Consider the following figure written in the form of a kōan (a short, paradoxical statement, often in the form of a couplet). Just like an actual Zen kōan, it is not designed simply to lead you to immediate enlightenment but rather to challenge you to meditate further to arrive at a deeper level of understanding.

The Passive Investing Yin Yang

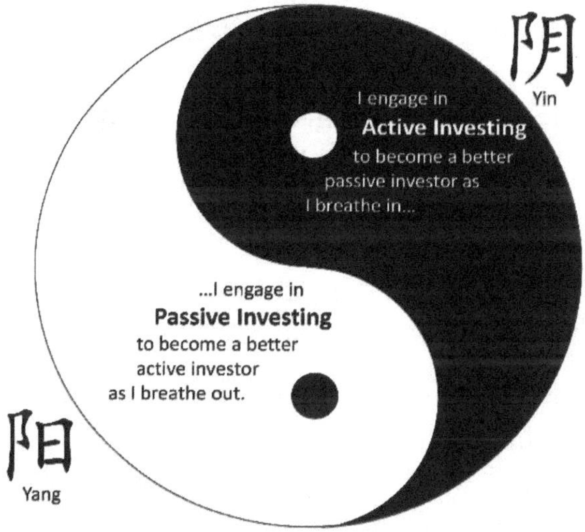

If you are one of those people who just didn't happen to be born wealthy or who doesn't already have a large nest egg, don't despair. There are still many things you can do if you don't have the capital to immediately deploy into passive income opportunities.

Invest Actively to Build Capital

A young girl once asked an old man on the streets of New York, "How do I get to Carnegie Hall?" His response? "Practice!" Though probably not the answer she was expecting, there is a timeless nugget of wisdom in the old man's response. If you do not currently have access to the sort of capital that can be readily converted into a convenient series of passive investments, your only choice other than "adding sweat" is to wait. You may have come to understand by this point in this literary that your author has many strong characteristics, patient waiting not being prominent among them.

If you would like to become an active real estate investor or business owner, this can be a great way to build capital at a quicker pace. There is a broad overlap between active and passive investors. The goal of becoming passive-income wealthy is generally a process of gradual growth whereby you slowly ramp down your active investments as you ramp up your passive investments.

Cut Expenses and Invest Your Savings

The only way to become wealthy is to live below your means. Say that three times! We can talk about increasing your passive income all day long, but if you allow yourself to fall prey to "lifestyle creep" by living an ever-richer lifestyle every time you have more money coming in. Cutting spending now will have a two-fold impact on your future by both accelerating the accumulation of wealth now and protecting your wealth from overspending later. The discipline you build will serve you more and more as you progress through your journey.

Consider the rule of 72 to estimate the impact of excess spending at age 25. Suppose you were able to cut $10,000 of spending this year, which you then invested at a 10% rate of return. Your money would double every seven years. Suppose you continue to work until you are 60. Your money would have doubled five times over the next 35 years for a total of 32x (2 x 2 x 2 x 2 x 2 = 32). Consider the impact of $320,000 on your lifestyle!

Learn a Six-Figure Skill

What about becoming an engineer or building some IT or finance skills? You don't necessarily need to go into debt to get the skills you need. There are many places that can teach you what you need for free. Khan Academy is great for math, IT, and much more. Hey, I didn't say it was going to be easy!

Gigging

We live in an age where it has never been easier to join the gig economy. If you happen to already have a six-figure skill like computer science, engineering or natural science, the opportunities for earning steady cash while you build your passionately active lifestyle can be a great adjunct. I am able to use my Ph.D. in microbiology to earn a six-figure income on the side of my real estate and other investments. I can work as little or as much as I like, which means that I can maintain my real estate professional status, which helps me greatly during tax season. If this sounds like you, check out Outlier and Remotasks. If you have skills in video editing, digital art, literature, accounting, or some other remunerable skillset, consider Upwork or Fiverr. Another way to create streams of passive income is to create courses on a site like Udemy.com.

Just as the roughly 1700 classic kōans were designed to break the human inclination to see the world in terms of duality, I hope that this kōan has made you more comfortable with existing in both worlds simultaneously.

Career Choices for Passionate Living

In almost any career there is enough downtime to enjoy life to the full – if only we could concentrate those moments into long enough stretches to do the things that light our individual fires.

Many jobs allow employees to travel for several days (or even months) in a row. The most well-known such job is teaching. Teachers in the US get their summers off. Nurses often work four ten-hour shifts each week and then enjoy a three-day weekend.

One freedom-producing job that is less well-known is firefighting. Depending on your municipality, you may be able to work two 24-hour shifts followed by four days off or even one 24-hour shift followed by 72 hours off. The training is very intense, in some cases sixteen weeks or more of full-time training. But, once you make the grade, you can more fully express your lust for life.

Depending on where you are in your journey, working a high-paying job may not be an option at the present moment. For example, you may currently be a student, or you may be in transition to go back to school. You may be able to find a job that leaves your mind free to build the knowledge and the passion that is growing within you each day. Are there any jobs that you can do right now that would give you that sort of mind freedom?

Many jobs, such as a desk-based security guard on a night shift or a parking attendant, may give you the freedom to grow the mind you need to take the next step as your very best self. Jobs that are performed at night or which require someone to be present at all times such as a receptionist or front desk hotel clerk, may work for you. Any job that has long periods of downtime between intense work sessions may also work. Some people find that time in jobs like working at a loading dock. Creative solutioning can go a long way toward bridging the gaps that separate you from the life you were meant to live. Don't stop at the first "no"!

Use The Capital you Already Have (Self-Directed IRA)

A self-directed IRA allows you to invest in substantially all of the alternative asset classes discussed in this book. Are you interested in investing in real estate or a startup company? Try doing that in your brokerage account, it isn't going to work.

Have you been working for a few years? You may have an IRA or a 401(k) with a substantial balance. How big is substantial? Considering that the minimum investment in many alternative investments, such as a syndication, is $50,000, you will probably want a multiple of this amount, considering the administrative fees required to keep your account open.

You don't have to invest all of your self-directed IRA cash in alternative investments immediately. Starting with a mix of traditional (e.g. equities) as well as alternative assets will give you time to learn and adjust as you ramp up alternative investments.

SIPC Protection

By allocating a portion of your IRA into a self-directed account, you're not just diversifying your portfolio but also safeguarding your funds from the potential financial distress of firms. The Securities Investor Protection Corporation (SIPC) offers a safety net, protecting up to $500,000 of value in each type of brokerage account per custodian. This means that if you had $500,000 in a Roth IRA, $500,000 in a traditional 401(k), and another $500,000 in a self-directed account, you could potentially be fully protected. This additional layer of protection can provide you with a sense of security and peace of mind.

What to expect: Anticipate a fun and exciting journey with your self-directed IRA. While setting it up may take a bit of effort and patience, the opportunities that it opens are tremendous. There is little to lose from setting up your self-directed IRA now if you are certain that you are going to use it. You should be able to invest in all of the assets that you currently invest in while you wait for the proper alternative opportunity. You should have no trouble holding nearly any asset mentioned in this book in a self-directed IRA with the possible exception of operating businesses.

You will want to be aware of the logistics involved in making these investments, which may not be quite as convenient as they are with your current online brokerage. For example, with my custodian, the purchase and sale of index fund shares is seamless. Purchasing shares of a corporation like Apple Inc. or Coca-Cola is also easy. However, if I want to sell the shares, I must transfer the shares to my broker to have the trade executed. For this reason, I choose to limit myself to index funds when I invest in the stock market in my self-directed IRA. When I find myself in possession of excess funds that I wish to invest in individual equities, I simply transfer the excess funds to my online brokerage and make the trades there.

Pitfalls: There are a few things that you will want to bear in mind as you prepare your first investment in a self-directed IRA. The first is the annual fees charged by the custodian, which can be substantial. Suppose the annual fee from your custodian is $2K. If you have a $50,000 investment that has a 20% IRR, that $2K per year fee will bring your investment returns down to 16%. That is all well and fine, but what if you don't have the money in the account to pay the fees? Most companies will allow you to use a credit card to pay your fees. I have been advised by a CPA that paying fees by credit card is not specified anywhere in the tax code, and although I have never heard of anyone getting in any trouble for paying by card, I pay my fees out of the account, just to be safe.

There are also many rules that you will need to follow when investing using a self-directed IRA, I will simply list the most common pitfalls. For example, you cannot lend any money to disqualified persons, which essentially includes you, your spouse, and anyone in your direct bloodline, such as parents, grandparents, children, or grandchildren. You cannot engage in any prohibited transactions like borrowing money from the IRA, using the IRA as security for a loan, or buying property for personal use.

Your Freedom Number?

Once you have enough passive income to cover your expenses, you have reached a stage known as "work optional." This rate of passive income is known as your "freedom number." Kōan #2: If you tie your freedom to a number in your mind, did you become free because you attained that number or because your mind released the number? You can become free the moment you release the number, don't wait. In this chapter, I will explore multiple resolutions to the paradox of freedom. If you are free, you can do whatever you want. But if you can do whatever you want, you can dream of literally anything your heart desires and allow yourself to become forlorn at the lack thereof. We have already explored becoming more active or using untapped capital, such as an IRA to achieve our passive income goals, as well as choosing an occupation that generates time freedom. Next, I will consider that the idea of freedom is just a concept in our minds. We become free the moment we choose to release our burdens.

There are several issues with the idea of a freedom number. As you become wealthy, you will have more time to learn, live, and grow. Your lust for life will naturally grow as you do, and the price tag is likely to grow along with it. This is why I have reservations about the concept. It encourages you to focus on life as a series of stages in which you first focus on accumulating a giant pile of poker chips expecting that you will be able to figure out what to do once you get there. The following quote from Olympic gold-medalist Michael Phelps sums it up for me "You can't put a limit on anything. The more you dream, the farther you get." Let's dream bigger together!

First of all, having been through this already, I guarantee that you can't fully know what you want to do until you start exploring this new world. This is why I recommend that you start exploring "freedom" or "retirement" early and gradually. If you are truly committed to living passionately, what you want to do will change and change again.

For example, I have enjoyed spending weeks on my small sailboat, which costs very little. A sailboat can go around the world on a single tank of gas. Since the family boat doubles as both travel and accommodations for my entire family, it can be very cheap. The dock fees for a 25-foot sailboat may be as low as $1.25 per foot ($31.25) per night, depending on the port and whether we are traveling in peak season. If it were just me, I could be quite happy with this life for months at a time. If you are married, you need to remember that it won't just be you adapting to your new life of freedom. You can think of each new hobby or vacation as a new "trial" retirement period. Retirement can be one of the most challenging times in a couple's love journey together. You don't want to face such an important transition as an "all or nothing" proposition. Better to test how you and your spouse react to it in small batches first.

I also enjoy the finer things in life, and the sailboat gets tiresome for my wife after a couple of weeks, so we make a point of programming some fine dining into the rhythm of the wind and waves to keep it fresh. An alternating rhythm of less-expensive travel modalities can help to keep the price tag down (and the sense of variety up).

The Three Poisons

If we are truly to understand the Zen of passive investing, we must start at the center of the *bhavacakra,* the Buddhist wheel of life. At the center of the wheel (see Figure X), we find the three poisons of (ignorance or delusion, attachment or greed, and aversion or hate) which consign the soul to an eternity of wandering the world. Let us examine each in turn.

Moha – Ignorance or Delusion (The Pig)

Proper investing is a matter of lifelong learning. There is simply no way that anyone could possibly know enough to be a good investor. The investing landscape is forever in flux; it is a moving target. At the same time, we must guard against the conceit that investing is all about technical knowledge. Far too many an investor has gotten the idea that knowledge equals wisdom. As Richard Feynman put it, "The first principle is that you must not fool yourself, and you are the easiest person to fool." During the go-go years of a bubble, many a great investor has failed not out of a lack of technical knowledge, but out of an inability to master one's own emotions. No less an intellect than Isaac Newton was caught up in the epic "South Sea Bubble." After losing a significant sum of money in the mania, he remarked, "I can predict the movement of heavenly bodies, but not the madness of crowds."

Rāga – Attachment or Greed (The Rooster)

The mania that grips investors often takes two forms: attachment and greed. Attachment is manifested through falling in love with a deal. When a deal seems to "pencil" but later is found to have unexpected issues that prevent it from performing as expected, what do you do? Do you "make the numbers work?"

or do you "go back to the drawing board"? Take three deep breaths and remind yourself that nothing is permanent. Your attachment to this deal will pass. Let it go. On the other hand, if you fail to let it go, the pain can be of long duration. Your attachment may not be permanent, but your poverty may be. Let it pass.

Another way to let go of a bad investment is to embrace *amor fati,* which is "love of fate" to borrow from another philosophy, the philosophy of stoicism. If the numbers don't work, love the fact that the numbers don't work. Feel yourself release the pain that would likely ensue from a bad or marginal deal. Realize that where you are is exactly where you are supposed to be in the universe. It is part of your journey. Accept that identifying a deal as marginal is good (because it illustrates that you have powers of discernment) or at least necessary (because not every project can be a home run). You are in the game - that is what counts.

Investments are like lovers. Some are good, some are bad, and some will drive you crazy. Even worse, some will make you want to fall in love at first sight. Investment is full of the same emotions that animate loving relationships - greed and lust. The danger is that we, as investors, often believe that we are operating in a rational world or in the rational portion of our brain, unlike matters of the heart. No matter how ugly it may be to admit it, we all tend to have an attachment to money that is stronger than we wish to admit. Money provides one-half of the potential energy for everything we wish to do (health being the other half). When we deal with money, we are very much dealing with matters of the heart. The only rational thing to do is to acknowledge our own irrationality. Only then can you avoid the investments that will drive you crazy.

As passive investors, we must remember that we should approach our deal much as active investors do. We may not personally perform all the due diligence that an active operator performs on a deal, but we should at least do enough research (and underwriting) to have answered the basic questions regarding each phase of due diligence.

We must also guard against greed. When yields decline as they have during most of the first quarter century of this millennium, the tendency to higher returns in risky assets often becomes insatiable. Low yields imply low interest rates, which means that these times foster projects of marginal quality that would not be funded during times of more normal interest rates. This means that at the time we observe the most dollars chasing investments, we see the greatest proportion of poor and marginal investments.

Suppose your neighbor just made a killing investing in Bitcoin, and you know he's dumber than you. Seeing this may make you angry and impatient, and that is natural. However, acting on such emotions, though very natural and human, is a recipe for disaster. Patience and deliberation are the keys to making sound decisions. Release the vain rooster of greed and attachment—let him go.

Dveṣa - Aversion and Hate (The Snake)

Like it or not, every human emotion, including aversion, has its sway in our investment world. Don't like numbers? You are letting aversion rule you. Are you bored with lease audits? Aversion has won. Don't believe that asset class X is worth learning about because you think that nobody is making money in that asset class now? Aversion wins again. No asset class is on top for long; that disliked asset class that you ignored will be on top one day, and if you are not paying attention, you will miss the bus.

The Three Poisons, which form the center of the Buddhist wheel of life (*bhavacakra*), can poison not only your investing but your life as well. The three poisons of ignorance (moha), depicted by the pig, attachment or greed (rāga), depicted by the rooster, and aversion (dveṣa), depicted by the snake, can keep your investing career in a state of wandering (saṃsāra).

The Three Antidotes

The three poisons may be ubiquitous, yet we are not left helpless. For the rooster of attachment and greed, we have generosity. For the feral pig of ignorance and delusion, we have education and wisdom. Finally, for the snake of aversion and hate, we have love and kindness. As we refocus our minds on the three antidotes, we turn towards a healthier and happier life while enjoying wider investing horizons.

It's...a Mirage

Once you truly grasp the ever-expanding nature of human desire, you will begin to see how the traditional concept of a "freedom number" is problematic. Further, once you discard the natural desire to see the world in terms of dualism, you open your mind to a wider world. Is freedom not having anyone around to ask you where you are going and when you will return? Or is freedom capturing the heart of the one you desire? When you are comfortable with the realization that it is both and neither at the same time, it becomes clear that freedom is all around us - it is infinite. It is only our own mind that causes us to feel unfree by desiring a state other than the one we currently occupy. We have as much freedom as our mind allows.

The beauty (and the fundamental problem) of the human mind is that it can imagine something better than that which currently exists. This ever-expanding desire can set us free, or it can become our prison. The Israelites knew well the destructive power of desire "Thou shalt not covet..." as it was set in stone three millennia ago. Thousands of years later, we still struggle...

Online Resources from George's Award-Winning Podcast "The Foundery – Where Leaders are Forged Daily"

Self-Directed IRA and Solo 401(k) with Damion Lupo

- Part I　　　　　　Part II

Invest in Yourself: The Ultimate Key to Financial Freedom!

"An investment in knowledge pays the best dividends."

- Benjamin Franklin

You wouldn't create a startup company, carefully write the business plan, raise the required capital, hire the right people, and then put off implementing the business plan indefinitely. These capital expenditures are crucial for business growth and increased exit valuation. So, why do we so often postpone our own personal growth?"

The #1 Capex Project is *You*!

To take an example from my business, the business of apartment ownership, in many cases the business plan is centered on the implementation of a more-or-less straightforward capex plan. We install new flooring, cabinets, countertops, landscaping, and we paint. Maybe we add a backsplash to the kitchen or a dog park. The value of the building increases with every improvement. Our investors benefit by getting greater cash flow earlier, which juices the IRR, which then benefits me as the operator by helping the project surpass its hurdles, which is how I earn my "promote," which is just a fancy way of referring to the money I earn for operating the property. With all of that riding on the implementation, do you think that I would risk lowering investor returns by waiting until "tomorrow" (which never comes) to implement my business plan? Of course not! And yet, we do it to ourselves every day. How sad!

Now is the perfect time to chart your personal investment roadmap to financial independence. Your strategy will vary based on your current position in the journey.

Suppose that you are young and talented but have no capital to invest. This would be a great time for you to find the six-figure skill that will propel you into the world of investment. If this example speaks to you, then ask yourself, "What steps do I need to take today, to obtain this six-figure salary?"

If you are already an investor but feel that you need to vastly increase the amount of capital that you have to invest, then ask yourself, "What is the most important thing I can do to become significantly more successful in my business today"? If you are an entrepreneur, I can almost guarantee that what will be most impactful is almost certainly exactly what you have been avoiding. Who can you reach out to that can help you figure out the next leg of your journey?

Quiz Time (no wrong answers)

I would like to

1. Lose weight
2. Complete my MBA
3. Establish a self-directed IRA
4. Other: ________________

Personal growth is absolutely essential to reaching your investment ambitions. Grow as a person and watch yourself grow as an investor. Compound interest works not only for money – it works even better when you apply it to yourself!

Steady as She Goes

How will you navigate towards your dream of passive income and a fulfilling life? As yours truly loves sailing, I find a nautical example apt. Imagine being at the helm of a sailing yacht where the object is to get to some wonderful but far-off place like a beautiful bay or an island. When the bearing (the direction the vessel is headed) matches the course (the direction the ship is to be steered), the captain gives the order "Steady as she goes" to let the helmsman know to maintain the course. However, the ship is rarely, if ever precisely, on course for more than a moment. The helmsman is constantly moving the captain's wheel to the left or right to maintain a constant bearing.

The Power of Iteration

Rather than bore you with stories from half a lifetime ago during my career in information technology, where the iterative approach is dominant and well-documented, I will pluck a tasty musical gem from the 1980s as an example. If any of you gentle readers happened to remember 1987, you couldn't possibly have missed seeing the video for "Here I Go Again" by Whitesnake from their self-titled album. The video was played incessantly, and the single reached #1 on the Billboard Hot 100. If you had MTV at the time, you can probably still remember Tawny Kitaen cartwheeling over the hood of a couple of Jaguar XJs in the well-worn video.

Well, unless you are a Whitesnake fan, you are far less likely to remember the 1982 version of the song. For fun, I went in search of the original version from the Saints and Sinners album, which, though much loved by fans, was released to far less fanfare. For the curious, I will list just a few of the differences between the singles to highlight the power of iteration. The original release featured a slower tempo and the characteristic

Hammond Organ sound of Deep Purple's Jon Lord rather than a more modern-sounding "dreamy synth," which dominated the 1987 version. The famous lyric "Like a drifter, I was born to walk alone" was originally "Like a hobo..." in the 1982 version. By the time the song made the hit parade, the song's co-author, Bernie Marsden, had already left for other projects. Success in any endeavor, just like the lyric in this hit song, is a "long and winding road." Don't be contented with simply making your investing career a great song - keep iterating until you come up with your #1 hit.

Ideally, you should plan your investing career in the same way. There is simply no way that you can dream what stage five should look like when you are at stage zero. Your ability to imagine a new life for yourself will expand as you grow. If you are exactly where you are supposed to be in five years, you aren't exercising your God-given creativity! Finding a life of true financial freedom through passive income will take many iterations. Think of your journey in terms of a "captain's logbook," as opposed to searching for a "cookbook." Throughout this journey, I am deliberately avoiding the notion that there is a single "A - B - C" progression. The goal is not to plan out your entire journey like a sea voyage. You want to change and adapt as the market and your goals evolve. As Dwight D. Eisenhower put it "plans are useless, but planning is indispensable." Each level of success or proficiency will allow you to make a better plan and dream a bigger dream as you crush the limiting beliefs that were present at the last stage. Think of the plan you are building more like a jazz ensemble than a classical music score.

A passive investing roadmap

Let's check in on what we have been learning and where we are headed next using the passive investing roadmap below. 1. We talked about choosing your asset classes in "Your Passive

Income Playbook: A World of Opportunity." 2. In "The Zen of Passive Investing," we discussed ways of building capital or unlocking the capital you already have. 3. Through combining steps "1" and "2," we are building our compound interest machine. 4. For reaching extreme goals like becoming extremely wealthy (if you aren't currently wealthy) or finding the time to fully enjoy your wealth (if you are), a program of continuous self-improvement is a must. Although this entire book deals with continuous self-improvement, I will discuss continuous self-improvement explicitly in "Arete." 5. Time to self-assess, how well are you enjoying the fruits of your labor? If your answer is later, I'm here to tell you that the time for anything is always now. Check "Don't Wait Until You Are Rich to Live the Active Life." 6. I will focus directly on dreaming bigger and bigger in "Building Your Active Lifestyle One Brick at a Time."

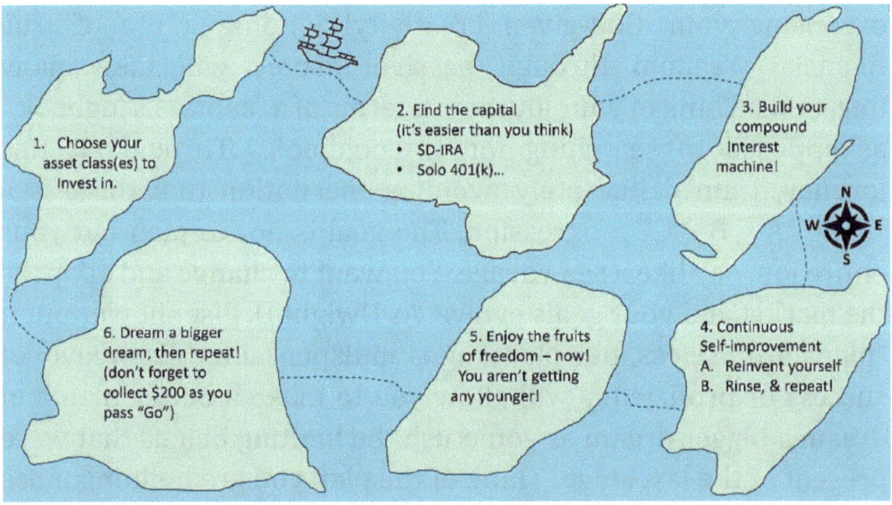

The most important part of executing any serious plan is the ability to iterate and pivot quickly. That is why this treasure map of the human soul is constructed in the form of a loop. As you pass "Go," remember that it is always a good time to reassess your asset allocations and make changes going forward.

Philosophical Corner

The Caterpillar and the Snake – An Allegory of Becoming

One day the snake was crawling on its belly through the forest. He looked up to an enchanted tree with lush foliage to see a caterpillar calmly eating a sumptuous leaf. The snake laughed and mocked the much smaller creature, who crawled on his belly just as he did but lacked his lithe grace and evident mastery of movement. "You are so pitiful and small; you will never be a majestic snake like me. You are lazy, staying in that tree all day, never bravely exploring the ground, and gliding rapidly across the terrain like me. Like all caterpillars, you will simply grow fat and then disappear." But the caterpillar, safe in the tree, paid the snake no mind and simply kept munching leaves. Over time, both animals grew and then shed their skin.

Many times, as the snake painfully rubbed his body against a firm rock to shed another layer of skin, he would think of the puny caterpillar and laugh to himself as he proudly remained slender even as he grew several times his original body length as he actively prowled the ground in search of fish, turtles, birds, and lizards. With each round of shedding, the snake became longer, faster as well as a better hunter. "Now that I have shed my skin, I shall capture larger prey," said he with pride. While the caterpillar, to his eyes, lazily grew fat on leaves.

Meanwhile, the caterpillar, rather than shedding his skin several times per year, did grow very fat, just as the snake observed. He grew so fat that he could crawl no further and began to rest on the leaf, unable to carry on. He became very sleepy, and his mind started to drift. For the first time, he began to wonder whether the snake was right. He had grown fat after all, just as the snake had predicted. Was it true that he was about to simply disappear?

One day, the snake passed by the same tree, but saw no caterpillar. He thought to himself, "Another fat caterpillar that just disappeared; perhaps he exploded from having eaten too many leaves. How sad that the caterpillar eats only stationary leaves while I, the powerful and dignified hunter stalk my quarry with skill and grace."

Fluttering above the snake, the once caterpillar, now a majestic and beautiful butterfly saw the snake still slithering

on its belly.

In the final analysis, there are two types of animals that crawl on their bellies and become plump enough to shed their skin. Whereas the caterpillar becomes a butterfly through growth, the snake simply becomes a larger snake. Snakes shed their skin between four and twelve times a year, only to remain on the ground. The butterfly faces a much more painful transition but only faces that transition once. The process of growth can be painful and awkward. This pain, however, is the entry price of a ticket to a new world of grace.

Let's reflect on this allegory of personal growth: the caterpillar and the snake both start by crawling on their bellies. While both shed their skin, the caterpillar transforms into a butterfly, but the snake merely becomes a larger snake.

In this allegory, the snake mistook the caterpillar, who, on a superficial level, was much like himself, for a defective snake. Throughout your journey, you may encounter many who don't understand your transformation. Rather than explain yourself, let your transformation speak. Focus on qualitative changes that unlock new possibilities. Make sure that you are growing in ways that open you up to new possibilities. The caterpillar wasn't content to simply crawl faster on the ground. You shouldn't be content either. Open your wings!

Play the Violin!

The "father of modern management," Peter Drucker, was once asked "how to become a better manager." His answer: "Play the violin." Cross-training your mind can have extraordinary benefits. Whether you choose the violin (or multivariable calculus, or dance, or...) matters little. What matters is that you continuously train your brain to do new things.

"No" is a Complete Sentence.

In addition to being grammatically correct, the above statement is key to finding the time to reach your extraordinary goals. Let's face it, the default in the modern world is to become occupied with tasks that don't directly serve our goals and our dreams. Without a willingness to put on the "brake," we end up rolling inevitably towards that default state where we are doing "everything" yet accomplishing little of what we set out to do.

Take a moment to list three to five things that you can immediately say "no" to without sacrificing productivity. News, politiblogs, binge-watching "The Bachelor," or a text message from your "friend" who is always complaining about how his life never changes are all things that you can safely say "no" to without consequence. The problems of the world will still be there. You can always "save the world" later. Have dreams of brokering peace in the Middle East or solving world hunger? Your opportunity to do all these things will wait for you.

Consider that dreams are like lovers. If you don't "take time to make time," they eventually attach themselves to someone else, leaving you sad, lonely, and blue. Don't let this happen! When something trivial pops up in the path of your dreams, consider the consequences of- blindly saying "yes" will have on your future. Taking time to envision this greater love in the future can help to give you the strength to say "no" to the relatively trivial demands of the present.

Put a Value on Your Time

The most straightforward way to put a value on your time is to divide all the money you have coming in by the amount of time it takes you to produce this value. I call this the "simple time value." As you grow your passive income, you can refine this calculation by considering the value-add that you create by investing in alternative assets vs. the S&P 500. We can call this the "refined time value."

Both of the above methods rely on past data. However, the true value of your time is what *today's* effort will produce. This is a number that can't yet be known. I propose that you estimate your true worth, a figure I refer to as your "present time value." If your goal is to grow (and it should be!) - you can set your time value at a figure that you believe you can reach within one to five years. I call this the "aspirational time value."

For me, the most convenient way of valuing time is to take my hourly pay as a freelance AI model trainer and say that absolutely any task that produces less than that hourly rate is already overdue for farming out to an employee or a freelancer. When seen in those terms, there are few tasks that can't be farmed out, given the pay differential between AI and administrative tasks.

Grow your Operation with a Virtual Assistant (VA)

As you become busier as an investor, you may find the time demands of being a successful investor creeping up on you. This can be a great time to consider hiring help. The price tag for these services is surprisingly low. You can easily hire a VA for $5 per hour or even less if you are willing to do the work of finding as well as hiring and firing. These tasks can be a job in and of themselves, so you may want to start with a VA service that handles these functions for you so you can get right down to tasking.

Once you are ready to send tasks to your VA, I have found that the quickest way to do this is through video. You should be able to find screen recording software for free (or for a nominal fee) that will allow you to record your voice and screen while performing repetitive tasks. Whether it is scheduling, email inbox management, drafting messages, etc., a VA can free you up in a major way! The goal here is to live free, not to live *for* free. Paying a little bit to make sure that your investing remains passive can be worth the investment you make.

Adding Concierges to the Mix

Concierges can greatly improve the passive quality of your entire lifestyle. Whether you need reservation assistance for dining, entertainment recommendations, or travel assistance, a concierge may be exactly what you need to get the job done without impacting your preferred activities or your sanity. Depending on what you are looking for, concierges can be found at many different price points.

Freelancers to the Rescue!

If you find the world of freedom available from hiring an assistant but are not ready to commit yet, a great way to "test the water" in terms of hiring and growing your business is to hire freelancers. As with a VA, many highly skilled tasks like market analysis can be farmed out to a freelancer. Many of the tasks required to publish this book, from editing to cover design, were performed by freelancers.

The major difference between a freelancer and a VA is that you have no commitment from task to task. If you have a task that needs to be performed once or perhaps a few times, it may be much more efficient to hire a freelancer.

The Lifestyle Creep Trap: Avoid Sabotaging Your Success

"Treat what you don't have as non-existent. Look at what you have, the things you value most, and think of how much you'd crave them if you didn't have them. But be careful. Don't feel such satisfaction that you start to overvalue them—that it would upset you to lose them."

- Marcus Aurelius

While it's important to enjoy the fruits of your labor, it's equally vital to ensure that additional income truly enhances your life. Without this balance, despite the added income, you might find yourself perpetually in the same financial situation with little to show for your efforts in the way of increased happiness and satisfaction in life.

If you notice that your spending habits haven't evolved as you build wealth and that you are simply buying luxury versions of things you already have (fancier clothes, nicer cars, or larger homes), it's time for a reality check. Consider how often you use these items, if you could live happily without them, and evaluate their true contribution to your happiness. Spend some time decluttering your closet, garage, or basement to confront the reality of your past purchasing decisions. You can also go through your Amazon orders page for a quick trip down memory lane. Try to correlate the amount of use an item received versus the way you felt when you purchased the item. Ponder your inability to accurately predict whether an item will become like your worn-out bag of golf clubs (if you like to golf) or like your not worn-out bag of golf clubs (if you *don't* often golf). All these purchases share one thing in common. They were *essential* to your happiness when you purchased them.

Resetting your "hedonic thermostat" can be a great way to speed up your journey towards financial freedom. When you look at your possessions from the standpoint of how much they actually contribute to your happiness, you may see shopping and the accumulation of "things" in a completely different light.

Don't think that I am bragging about my ability to accurately predict the value of a purchase to my life upfront. As I mentioned in the opening paragraph, as a data scientist, I make predictions for a living (as a joke). *And I still don't get it right.* If you are a shopaholic (I can be at times, and will share my shopping weaknesses below), it is time to confront your demon!

Lifestyle Creep Avoid letting lifestyle creep consume your passive income as in the left side of the figure. Like the Red Queen, you will find yourself running faster and faster just to stay in one place. Instead, reinvest your wealth to gain more time and resources for further investments and for personal growth to ensure that your financial journey remains progressive and sustainable.

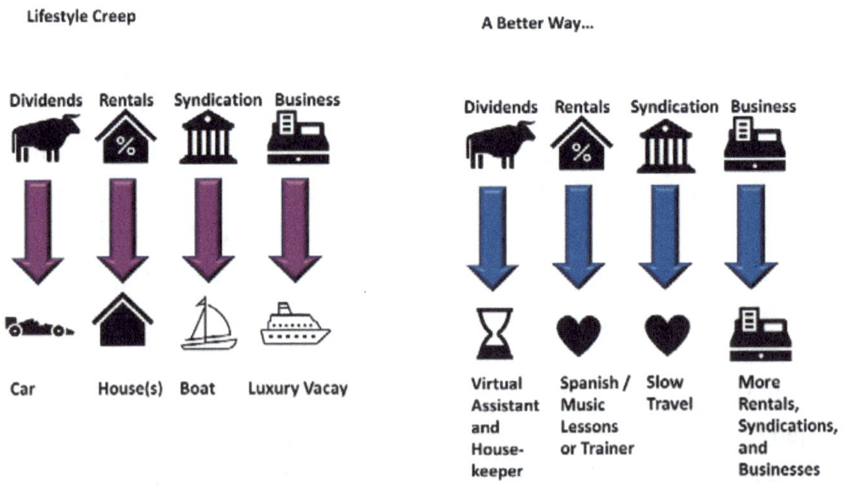

Philosophers' Corner

Shoppers Reality Check – The Three Sieves for Savvy Shoppers

1. Will I use it?
2. Where will I put it?
3. Is it necessary?

Before making a purchase, ask yourself these three questions: Will I use it? Where will I put it? Is it necessary? If you struggle to answer any of these questions, you might be better off saying 'no' to the item. Additionally, consider if the purchase can wait. These filters can help you make more conscious and satisfying choices.

If the "shoppers reality check" sounds dimly familiar, I based it vaguely on the apocryphal three sieves of Socrates. The story goes as follows: When a man approached Socrates with something he just couldn't wait to get off of his chest, Socrates sensed that he was about to hear gossip or negativity. He asked the man "Are you certain that what you are about to say is true?". The man replied sheepishly that he had overheard the rumor and couldn't be absolutely certain of its veracity. Socrates next asked the man, "Is it kind?". The man, now a bit chastened, replied, "No, I am sad to say." Finally, Socrates asked the man, "Is it necessary?" The man, now silent and head bowed in shame, simply walked away.

As promised, here are my shopping weaknesses. I tend to overspend on men's clothing and jewelry. Often, my new clothes sit unworn for long periods, and the jewelry I buy for my wife remains in the closet, sometimes for years, until a special occasion arises. While there may be some redeeming value in planning ahead for gifts, the habit of overstocking my wardrobe is less justifiable. We all have room for growth!

Are you ready for an exercise? As you navigate your day tomorrow, ponder during your quiet moments the "price tag" of each experience. To take one representative day, the best memories involved taking my older son to Urbain Air ($19.99 per month) for pizza and trampoline fun, followed by a park (free) where I watched him play while writing this book. The next week, the most memorable experience was cooking with my younger son, followed by taking both of my sons to my in-law's house to do some plumbing and landscaping (lawn bags at $0.50 each plus a brass drain cap for $1.59). As you try this exercise on your own, you may be surprised at just how true the old cliché is: "The best things in life are free." If spending a dollar doesn't bring you happiness, don't sacrifice your financial freedom to do it.

The three sieves of Socrates (discussed in the sidebar above) "Is it true, is it kind, is it necessary?" are great not just for philosophers with strange facial hair[5] but for everyday living as well.

---

[5] If you are wondering upon whom the "strange facial" hair of my avatar in the blue box is styled, it is after the Chinese philosopher Mencius (Mengzi 孟子). "Master Meng" believed that the government should take a "hands-off" approach to government, that the government should prevent monopolies, and that taxation should be minimal. Your humble author believes these things as well.

Passive Income, Happiness, and Scientific Research

Research supports the idea that money alone doesn't bring lasting happiness. Concepts like 'hedonic adaptation' and the 'hedonic treadmill' explain why people often return to their previous level of happiness after significant life changes such as winning the lottery or a terminal diagnosis. However, sustainable increases in happiness can be achieved through acts of kindness, suggesting that using financial freedom to help others can lead to a more fulfilling life.

Research supports the idea that money alone doesn't bring lasting happiness. Researchers use the terms "hedonic adaptation" and "hedonic treadmill" to refer to the phenomenon that people who experience either positive or negative life-changing events such as winning the lottery, or a terminal diagnosis often return to roughly their former level of happiness after a short period of time although there is some "stickiness" to the newly achieved happiness[6].

So, you may wonder, if this is a book about "passionate living," how can the author believe that we can live more passionately through passive income if happiness is unchanging and unchangeable? Well, it turns out that there is a way to make a lasting change in your happiness level and it isn't directly through money. The catch is that you will have to use your financial freedom to do something nice for someone else! Subjects in one study who performed random acts of kindness one day each week experienced sustainable increases in happiness[7].

---

[6] Bottan, Nicolas Luis and Perez-Truglia, Ricardo, Deconstructing the Hedonic Treadmill: Is Happiness Autoregressive? (October 1, 2009).

[7] Sheldon, K., & Lyubomirsky, S. (2004). Achieving sustainable new happiness: Prospects, practices, and prescriptions. In P. A. Linley & S. Joseph (Eds.)

(Further) Lessons from the Lottery

Before we leave the issue of the impact of wealth on happiness, studies of lottery winners have produced decidedly mixed results. The idea that winning the lottery has no positive impact on happiness is at least as old as Philip Brickman's famous 1978 research[8] contrasting lottery winners and accident victims with "normal" controls.

More recent research has produced mixed results. The idea that happiness regresses to the mean following a windfall event is backed by the 2009 study on life-changing events previously cited above[5]. A 2019 study of German lottery winners showed an increase in satisfaction with life which was particularly marked for the largest winners[9]. A 2020 survey of Swedish lottery winners 5 and 22 years after their windfall found "sustained increases in overall life satisfaction that persist for over a decade, and which show no evidence of dissipating over time"[10].

As far as the health effects of wealth, it appears that where the study is done has much to say about the impact. A Singaporean study found improvements in health in lottery winners in contrast to studies in Western European countries, which do not generally find improvements in health, attributed by the authors

---

[8] Brickman, P., Coates, D., & Janoff-Bulman, R. (1978). Lottery winners and accident victims: Is happiness relative? Journal of Personality and Social Psychology, 36(8), 917–927 https://doi.org/10.1037/0022-3514.36.8.917

[9] Oswald, Andrew and Winkleman, Ranier "Lottery Wins and Satisfaction: Overturning Brickman in Modern Longitudinal Data on Germany" in *The Economics of Happiness: How the Easterlin Paradox Transformed our Understanding of Well-Being and Progress*. Edited by Mariano Rojas (Springer, 2019)

[10] Erik Lindqvist, Robert Östling, David Cesarini. Long-Run Effects of Lottery Wealth on Psychological Well-Being. The Review of Economic Studies, Volume 87, Issue 6, November 2020, Pages 2703–2726, https://doi.org/10.1093/restud/rdaa006

to the strong social safety nets in these countries[11]. For example, a British study found a significant improvement in mental, but not physical health. The lack of a positive impact on physical health despite an increase in mental health may be attributed to the higher amount of social drinking and smoking among this population[12].

What can I say? Social sciences aren't exact sciences like physics or chemistry. We can't expect research to provide us with a precise prescription detailing how to live a meaningful life like the Laws of Newtonian Physics. We will have to draw our own conclusions while using our common sense, intuition, and values to guide us. Of course, money doesn't buy happiness. However, it does help us avoid the misery of poverty. The degree to which it enhances our life is up to us and the mindfulness of our choices.

---

[11] Seonghoon Kim, Kanghyock Koh J Health Econ. 2021 Mar:76:102414. The effects of income on health: Evidence from lottery wins in Singapore https://pubmed.ncbi.nlm.nih.gov/33387919/

[12] Benedicte Apouey, Andrew E Clark Health Econ. 2015 May;24(5):516-38.. Winning big but feeling no better? The effect of lottery prizes on physical and mental health. https://pubmed.ncbi.nlm.nih.gov/24677260/

Preparing for the Permanent Vacation

"Life would be infinitely happier if we were born at the age of eighty and gradually approach eighteen."

- Mark Twain

Retirement is a place we all hope will last many decades. Although we all expect it to be a wonderful place, we have little idea of what it may look like, because we haven't bothered to check out the travel brochure, much less having actually visited it to see if we like it.

You wouldn't commit to living somewhere for ten, twenty, or thirty years without checking it out first. So, why do people put off testing their retirement until they are already there? By that time, it is already too late to make adjustments. Suppose you don't have enough money to live your dreams. It isn't easy to budget for something you haven't even planned. What if you miss the feeling of importance your old job provided? You don't want to be stuck between the opportunity of the new and the comfort of the old. By taking a gradual approach, we can avoid many of the pitfalls that so commonly befall the poorly planned retirement.

There are two approaches to testing freedom, and with a nod to Hemingway, I suggest you try them in this order, "first gradually, and then all of a sudden." Testing the retired life gradually allows you to enjoy the fruits of your considerable labor and while helping you spur you on to even greater achievement. Remember the metaphor of the ripples in the pond. Don't hold onto the stone! Toss it now with all your living strength. You always have your entire life ahead of you. However, you will never have more life ahead of you than you have at this present moment.

Avoiding Common Retirement Mistakes: Planning Ahead for Fulfillment and Security

No Plan at All

Retirement should be a time to pursue your wildest dreams rather than a time for falling asleep in your soup. Most people have some vague idea about rekindling their interest in their hobbies and catching up with all their old friends from high school (which will never happen, by the way). The time to catch up on your hobbies is *now*, while you plan your retirement so that your days will be loaded with fulfillment and enjoyment, not existential panic.

Consider what hobbies you may pursue with more time in the future, but don't wait for that ill-defined "tomorrow" to get started. Beta-test your plan now, so that your future is ready for flight as the time and money appear.

A Poorly Planned Budget

"We won't need as much money when we are retired because we won't have a house payment, and the kids will be on their own." Unless you plan to spend your retirement watching Netflix and eating microwave popcorn, you should expect to spend *more*, not less, during retirement.

Adjusting Expectations (It's Different Than I Remembered...)

I once envisioned a life for myself of enjoying life on a tropical island with days of scuba diving and evenings of Piña Coladas. Sadly, I realized that eardrums are among the parts of the body that age and become less useful over time. I am still able to dive, but alas, it isn't as I remembered it in my younger days when I could effortlessly equalize the pressure of my eardrums. Nowadays, I prefer shore diving, which allows me to equalize slowly as the depth increases gradually, rather than diving from a boat. You may find that your dreams change too, as you live your passion (or as you grow older).

Further, I found that the sun isn't great for my Finnish complexion and that alcohol hits a lot harder with the advancing years, particularly given the strict diet I maintain to keep my arthritis at bay so that I can dance. You may wonder what became of the spa days I would send my wife on. Well, after her good friend got hepatitis during the after-dinner spa day debrief, there haven't been any spa days since. When I say that your "retirement" will change and change again, I mean that if you play your cards right it will change continuously like a kaleidoscope.

In 2024, my plans changed again, as I decided to leave my precious Sally Mae "on the hard" for a year while I pursued other interests, namely Argentine tango and Spanish lessons. This is also the year that I left my workaholism behind or at least adopted a much healthier approach to work. Of course, if you asked my wife, she would claim that I am still a workaholic. What can I say? Opinions differ. Oh, well, baby steps...

If you think that a lifetime of champagne and cruise ships is in your future, it is better to try it out now to see how you like that style of living now in small quantities. If you decide it isn't what you want, you will have that much more time to hatch a new plan.

Wait, I've Had Enough Fun Already!

You may find that after spending three weeks in paradise that some form of "work" actually suits you and that leisure isn't truly what you wanted after all. Self-knowledge is a fundamental part of living a fulfilling life. You will come back to "work" stronger than before. Of course, this is exactly what I expect given the sort of people who have worked hard enough to become free from work in the first place. Better to discover the proper mix of work and play now than to find yourself drowning in a sea of too much time on your hands.

Differentiating "Wealth" vs. "Riches": The Key to a Sustainable Retirement

Being wealthy and being rich sound similar, so why is the distinction so important? Having the wherewithal to pursue your dreams of living actively on passive income requires that you understand the distinction and that you decide to be wealthy rather than simply rich. The designation "Rich" simply refers to assets and outward display. A person who dresses in fancy clothes, lives in a large house, and can afford the monthly payment is "rich," but are they "wealthy"? Many such rich people are rich at only the most superficial level, living at or even above their means. They may be in every bit as precarious a position as their less-rich neighbors if they lose their jobs or become ill.

To be wealthy, on the other hand, you need to live below your means. There is simply no other way to do it. If you spend every dime that comes in, it will never matter how much money you have coming in, your situation will never fundamentally change. You will continue to live hand to mouth. A wealthy mindset focuses on many things that are not common among the non-wealthy, such as using wealth as capital to build more wealth or to fundamentally transform one's circumstances and a habit of generous giving. On the other hand, rich people often spend their money in a way that passes right through them.

Rich people see money in much the same way as the middle class which is why they still aren't wealthy. They still live hand to mouth, only in fancier surroundings. Becoming wealthy requires a significant mindset shift. If you think that "stuff" will make you happy, take a walk down memory lane by cleaning out your garage, basement, or your closet. Every purchase from a guitar, a book, a coat, or a pair of dance shoes is made with high hopes of being "just the thing" to complete our lives. So many of these things fall into almost immediate disuse. Part of the mindset shift to wealth is to break out of the cycle of thinking that a purchase will "complete our lives." The wealthy see money for what it is – simply a tool. Focusing on money as capital will help you to see money as a tool, and it will help you to make the choices that you will need to make.

In fact, many wealthy people carry things a bit too far. The attitudes that generate wealth are often the same attitudes that lead the wealthy to fail to spend their money on even the most basic of necessities. Particularly among the first-generation wealthy, it is not uncommon to see wealthy people going around with holes in their clothing. I hope that my gentle readers do take a portion of their wealth to ensure basic comfort. At the same time, I hope the message is clear – uncommon results are created by uncommon people. If you want to enjoy true wealth, you aren't likely to find it or keep it without uncommon attitudes towards money.

Financial Milestones: Setting Goals for a Secure Retirement

Are you willing to forego a little luxury today, to have the capital to live like you dreamed of tomorrow? It helps to have a milestone to aim for. Something that will help keep you on track. Considering the common minimum for investing in a real estate syndication is often $50,000 you could set that as your goal. Let me be clear: one real estate syndication, even an extraordinarily successful one, isn't going to change your life, even though it may be a very important step along the way. One of my favorite investors of all time, Charlie Munger sets the bar at $100,000. "The first $100,000 is a bi$$h, but you gotta do it, I don't care what you have to do – if it means walking everywhere and not eating anything that wasn't purchased with a coupon, find a way to get your hands on $100,000". Regardless of where you set the first marker on your path of 10,000 miles, it is important to set goals along the way and to celebrate when you reach a goal. Don't forget to celebrate your progress. A good day is a day that you faithfully execute your plan with discipline. Results come when they are ready to come. Don't focus on the scoreboard, focus on how you are training. If you train like a champion and are prepared to take feedback and pivot, when necessary, you will win more than you will lose. And that is far more than most people can say. Commit to the first step today.

Time to take out your pencil, pen, or crayon and write in this book!

I commit to having my first ($__00,000) by (___ / ___ / 20__)

Closing Thoughts on Transitions

Few things go well the first time, retirement being no exception to the rule. My experience suggests taking a more iterative approach to leisure is healthier. My hope is that you are able to make the passage from the workaday world to retirement a gradual transition rather than a crash landing as it often turns out to be.

The World is Your Oyster: Don't Wait Until You're Rich!

"There is no time like the present."

- Traditional

If you think that becoming rich will solve your problems, think again. Although having money does not bring happiness, poverty, bills, and debt can (and do) bring misery. Consider all the people who never have the good fortune to live to the mythical retirement age of 65. Don't wait to live your dream. There is a far better reason to not wait than the fact that you may not live to 65. You deserve to live today. If you think you must wait to pursue your dream until you retire, the odds are that you will find some other excuse not to live passionately tomorrow.

Living large is no different than anything else. Practice makes perfect. Whatever you see as passionate living today is only leading to a higher vista that will allow you to see even further. This is an iterative process in which you build a more passionate life at an exponentially increasing rate like the nautilus builds its radiating spiral shell outward. We simply can't skip steps here. Your radiating spiral of passionate living depends on prior steps just like the outer layers of the shell depend on the inner layers of the shell.

The goal of this chapter is to cater to the spirit of adventure on a variety of budgets. By the end of this chapter, you will never need to use "it's too expensive" as an excuse not to live your life to its fullest potential.

Philosophical Corner – Waiting for Godot

Don't buy into the traditional notion that life is to be lived in two phases. Namely, saving for retirement and then putting up a sign on your front door saying "gone fishing" so to speak. This is what our traditional education has drilled into our brains. This approach is broken. Let's discard that old and broken philosophy for a philosophy that is more befitting of the adventurous types that pick up books on investing and entrepreneurship (like you!). This book isn't just about making a ton of money (well, it is about that too); it is about living a life of growing passion as you take the financial bull by the horns. If you wait until "retirement age" to cut loose and focus on what makes your heart happy, you will find yourself a beginner at a point at which you should already be an expert. Let your friends wait for the proverbial Godot. Take financial action today. And just one more thing before we close this grey box. When you tell your friends this story about how it's finally time to stop waiting and just buy George's book already, make sure you put the stress on the first syllable. Its GOD-oh, not Guh-DOH.

Next, let's explore multiple options designed to fit your budget as you morph from investor to passive income superstar!

Slow Travel vs. Fast Travel

The internet has opened the opportunity to enjoy destinations for longer periods of time to more people. Enjoying an exotic destination for extended periods need not involve hostels or backpacking if you are still on a budget. From weekly discounts on short-term rentals to renting a flat for a month at a time, you can find many ways to save a lot by planning better and staying longer. You may find that you enjoy the experience enough to join the ranks of the digital nomads who continue to enjoy the benefits of favorable currency exchange rates as well as the benefits of cultural immersion.

The slow traveler focuses on cultural experiences and quality interactions with locals rather than hopping from one expensive hotel to another. Having passive income frees you from the treadmill of having only a couple of weeks to enjoy a destination during the busiest season and having to rush to make it happen, which will push you into the more expensive hotels in town. On the other hand, if you are focused on cultural experiences and willing to plan, you may find yourself comfortable a little bit outside the major cities where English is less widely spoken and where local knowledge becomes more valuable. By taking time to understand the culture and plan, the slow traveler finds other ways to save money, such as traveling during the off-season and transportation. Passive income frees you to travel when you want. You can fly in and out on a Wednesday or a Thursday which can save a bunch.

Saving on accommodations begins with living like a local. You can rent an apartment for a month and pay less than you would for a week in a hotel, but you will have to know the local language and work a little to make this happen. Self-cooked meals (if you are in an expensive destination) can help considerably as well.

Experienced travelers know to ask for a monthly discount for short-term rentals. It isn't listed, so you won't find out unless you ask. Traveling light can also help to simplify the experience. If you are staying in an apartment or a short-term rental, much will be provided. How many outfits do you really need if you can do your own laundry? Homestays are another great way to keep the expense of a trip down while keeping the cultural intensity up. A homestay allows you to fully experience the culture by living in the home of a local.

Another great way to save money is to call your preferred hotel directly (rather than using some third-party online booking service) and ask for a direct booking discount. Like so much in life, if you don't know to ask, nobody will tell you.

Ground travel can also be much cheaper by buying a weekly or monthly bus or subway pass. You can save a ton on a rental car by using a peer-to-peer car-sharing marketplace. Unlike the expensive, mint-condition cars you get from a traditional car rental, you can find some extraordinary deals if you are willing to take a car that is just a few years old. If you enjoy driving a manual transmission automobile, you can find that with a peer-to-peer rental, which is something you won't find at any of the main rental companies. Enjoy off-roading? Don't plan on taking a car from one of the main rental companies on anything unpaved. But if you do plan to go off-road, be sure to carefully check the requirements of both the car sharing marketplace as well as the owner of the car you are renting. Voiding your insurance can be expensive.

Handling your electronic gadgets abroad takes some...adapting. Cell phones can also be very expensive abroad. Make sure that your phone can accept a local SIM card before you leave home. Gadgets can be very power hungry, so make sure that you have all the cables and adapters before you leave. Alternatively, you can just purchase a new charger when you arrive, which will save some space.

If you plan to stay away from home for an extended period, you will also need to consider plans for healthcare. Getting some routine procedures while abroad can help to defray or even zero out the cost of the trip. On the other hand, you may feel better with medical evacuation insurance and international health insurance, which can be surprisingly cheap. You may want to consider the likelihood of actually using medical evacuation insurance. If you are traveling an ocean away, the time and costs associated with leaving and returning may make it a better option to be treated locally.

Passion and Pain - Medical Care While Abroad

When traveling the world, especially for extended periods, injury and sickness are a distinct possibility. Basic medical insurance abroad can be obtained at a very reasonable price from various companies like SafetyWing or World Nomads. For daredevils, these plans cover adventure sports and other dangerous activities to provide peace of mind. These services also provide coverage for other issues travelers face, including trip interruption, lost baggage, damaged electronics, natural disasters, and more.

At the time of this writing, SafetyWing will insure individuals up to the age of 69. Individuals between 10 and 39 can get four weeks of coverage for $56.39, and world travelers of age 60 to 69 can be covered for $196.84. Adding adventure sports to the mix covers 34 activities, from aviation, boxing, and cave diving to skiing, skydiving, and SCUBA diving. The addendum costs only $10.00 regardless of age bracket. Best of all, you can add two children to the policy for free.

For more extensive coverage, you can check into World Nomads. For example, a 35-year-old traveler to South America for one month can be covered for around $169. World Nomads covers 200 dangerous activities in its base plan. If you are contemplating running with the bulls, wingsuit flying, or shark cage diving, you can add the explorer plan for peace of mind.

Sampling a Life of Romance and Luxury - *Now*!

Suppose your retirement dream is to relocate to Buenos Aires and spend the rest of your days living like a porteño, enjoying Malbec, and dancing the tango with the woman or man of your dreams (why not dream big?). You don't have to wait for the plane to touch down to enjoy the amazing power of the US Dollar. With the internet and a couple of minutes with your favorite search engine, you can have a live Spanish tutor show you all the ins and outs of the language from "che" to "chau" for just a few dollars an hour (and believe me, the Spanish they speak around the Rio de la Plata is not the Spanish you learned in high school). You will also find that you can save on currency exchange through the unregulated "blue rate" currency exchanges, which offer a hefty premium over the official "red rate" currency exchanges due to currency controls.

Sampling the active life as you build passive income will help you get a handle on your budget and can also help sustain the motivation required to get you there.

Adventure Travel

Who says that slow travel can't be fast-paced? If you have a more adrenaline-driven or athletic bent to your personality, there are nearly limitless possibilities for 4-wheeling, rock climbing, hiking, white water rafting, or canyoneering. Adventure travel is one way to enjoy life to the max while avoiding a Michelin 3-star price tag.

Worry-Free International Travel

There are several ways to avoid bad situations while abroad by thinking ahead. You can avoid issues with documents being lost or stolen by taking a picture, and also by making a photocopy in case your cell phone is stolen. Breaking in your shoes before you leave is another great idea for international travel or even if you are just going as far as Disneyland. Packing light is another great idea that becomes much more feasible if you get into the habit of doing your own laundry or availing yourself of the hotel laundry service. An add-on benefit of traveling light is that you have room in your suitcase for that "must have" item that you found along the way. A few plastic bags to organize small items and to separate the dirty laundry from the clean can make traveling much more convenient. Sunscreen is always great to have, and don't forget the earplugs, particularly if you are traveling with children.

The frequent traveler will want to keep an electronic packing checklist that can be printed out anew for each type of adventure. For example, my wife keeps a special list just for sailing. Items like canned grape leaves and cell phone power packs are particularly tailored to the tight quarters and long hours away from restaurants and grocery stores experienced on sailing trips. Believe it or not, many marinas offer showers, but not soap or shampoo, and you can be 100% certain that towels are definitely not included.

Passionate Living ($)

If your budget is low, here are many suggestions for travel and adventure on a budget.

Cultural Travel (you can also use these ideas for trip prep or for a "staycation")

Whether you are currently at liberty to travel freely at this point in your life's journey, there are many things that you can do to bring the excitement, even if you need to stay close to home for the time being. If traveling the world is your dream, but you aren't able to start just yet, a cultural adventure is still within reach. Whatever region of the world you are interested in, you can easily learn their music, folkloric dance, cuisine, and language, all without leaving town. We'll cover some of the ways you can do this in the following sections.

Dance

One of the greatest and most affordable adventures of my life has been dance. Are you fascinated by the sexy bachata rhythms of the Dominican Republic? What about the exciting salsa rhythms of Puerto Rico, Cuba, and beyond? Learning about the music and dance of a culture can be a great way to enhance an upcoming trip (or to simply enhance your evenings). An unlimited lesson card can cost $150 for a month or even less. What you can learn in a month of dance from a talented instructor is worth far more! You may wonder why dance schools offer such an amazing deal. Clearly, most people are tied to the W-2 ball and chain and can't avail themselves of more than a few lessons a week. With my passive income streams, I can easily make it to 40 lessons in a month (and possibly more if the studio offers several classes in an evening). At a rate of less than $4.00 per group lesson, you can't say that it is an overly expensive hobby. The trick is to gain control of your schedule.

With intensive study over the last seven months, I am already preparing for my first dance competition. For those who, like me, find themselves needing to stay close to home while raising children, an adventure like dance may be just right!

Language

If you are like me, you know the frustration of spending countless hours and untold expense on a university language course or online learning courses only to find that seemingly endless effort leaves you falling far short of the conversational level. With technology today, there is no reason that you - yes, you can be conversational in a foreign language in a matter of weeks to months.

For me, nothing can compare with the sound and feel of Argentine Tango. With passive income, I am not only able to indulge in my favorite hobby, but I am also able to augment it in amazing ways as well. As preparation for a slow-travel trip to Argentina, I have been taking Castellano Argentino (pronounced cast-eh-**zhan**-oh ar-hen-**teen**-oh) lessons, but we can call it Argentine Spanish here since that is easier to pronounce. By hiring a local tutor and using technology, I am able to practice conversational Spanish with a live instructor for $10 per hour!

At a pace of 12 hours per month, my progress has been rapid. I am already able to travel with confidence after just a few months. My first few lessons involved end-to-end usage of Google Translate. Within eight weeks, I found myself chatting quite confidently. There is simply no quicker way to become conversational than to engage in...conversation. In the same time frame, I could have spent several times that amount on a university course for a fraction of the benefit.

If budget is a concern, it is possible to get a tutor for much less than $10 per hour. Did I mention that my Argentine Spanish teacher is a cultural history professor who specializes in cultural travel? You just can't make this stuff up! If you haven't taken the time to explore this world of opportunity, you may be surprised by the range of options available.

There are also services like Baselang that allow you to get monthly unlimited one-on-one tutoring for $185 as of this writing! Once you get past the idea that money is the limiting factor, scheduling becomes the key to success in your globetrotting ambitions.

Tips for Personal Growth on a Budget

With the internet, finding an instructor to cost-effectively prep you for your trip is easy. The profusion of tutoring sites makes learning almost any skill potentially cheap. The only catch is that your instructor will need to be from a country with a low cost of living so that your dollar will go far. Well, there may be one other catch, you may have to speak the local language to avail yourself of the opportunity. I won't try to list all of the sites that offer such tutoring since they tend to be quite new and are thus likely to change over time. Just start your search by finding cultures and countries that have low GDP that you have an interest in.

If speaking a language other than English is not your thing, consider an African tutor. Africa features English speakers and great exchange rates. You can find all of the countries currently served by Superprof at https://www.superprof.com/superprof-in-the-world.html. Please be advised that hyperlinks often change so if this doesn't work for you, you can try searching for "Superprof Countries" or something of that nature. Currently, Superprof has tutors available in South Africa and Nigeria. You may also try to find an English-speaking tutor in a non-English-speaking country, although this will be hit-or-miss. With time zones ranging between 5 and 8 hours ahead of Eastern Standard Time, it is easy to pick a convenient time.

So, how great of a deal can you get considering the USD exchange rate? As of this writing in 2024, if you are considering a

Nigerian tutor, the USD to Naira exchange rate is 1515 meaning that a Nigerian tutor that charges ₦5,000 (5,000 naira) per hour can be hired for under $4.00 per hour. You can get similar quality deals from South African tutors.

For those who work out at home, a remote personal trainer is already ideal. As for me, my entire basement is divided between gym and dance. I appreciate the flexibility of teleconferencing my trainer so that I don't have to commute to the gym. With personal trainers in the US easily costing between $50 and $120 per hour, the cost savings can be significant.

Life coaching and high-performance coaching can bring extraordinary benefits to the sort of highly motivated individuals who seek to build passive income. With the price tag exceeding $100 per hour, it can be difficult to find the money early in your career. Enter technology! There is no reason to wait when you can find an experienced coach that easily fits your budget. For even $10 per hour, you can find a coach that will help you clarify and reach your goals. In many cases, your first lesson is free.

Other Ways to Benefit from Overseas Teachers (and the Power of "King Dollar")

Online tutoring is not limited to music, dance, and personal training. You can also find great classes for other fields such as art and design, as well as academic fields. If you are still in school, consider the time you can free up by getting an academic tutor for yourself or your children.

Passionate Living ($$)

If you have a bit to spend but don't consider yourself "rich" yet, here are some ideas to light the fire of "passion" in your life!

Sailing

For a longer-term adventure on a budget, consider a small sailboat for family fun. For a few thousand dollars, you can buy a sailboat large enough to sleep on. With no diesel bill and dock fees, your only major "splurge," you can sail to an anchorage near an island (or coastal) paradise and stay for free. With a small inflatable dinghy, you can enjoy all that your destination has to offer and sleep for free each night on your own boat-el!

Travel Hacks - Maximize the Excitement on any Budget!

Hotels that have had recent "image issues" or that are looking to maintain full occupancy without cheapening their image by publicly displaying low prices sometimes offer to be listed on "blind booking" services. With blind booking, you don't get to find out the name of the hotel you will be staying at until after you book.

If a short-term rental is more your style, you can still get great deals by contacting your host directly and asking for a 25% discount. In return, you can show past reviews you have made in the past and promise to write a similar glowing, detailed review. You can also pledge a small gift, such as a small bottle of wine, to be left after the stay and let the host know that you will be leaving the place in immaculate condition.

Getting the best price on plane tickets requires outsmarting the pricing algorithms that are designed to squeeze you for all you are worth. If you live in a high-GDP country, these algorithms take into account the fact that you are likely to be able to pay more. Searching for similar flights tends to bring a higher price the second time around. You can protect yourself using a free VPN. Don't fall for the myth that a private browser will make you "invisible" to airlines. The only thing that incognito mode does is discard your history. While this can be valuable in terms of avoiding the cookie that indicates you made a similar search earlier, the airlines can still see your IP address in private browsing mode.

Here is a tip for travelers desiring extra "elbow room" without additional cost. If you travel as a pair, you can try booking the window and the aisle seat. Unless the flight is booked solid, or a solo traveler chooses the middle seat, you have a decent likelihood of having an empty seat between you. Good luck!

You can use the algorithm's pricing patterns based on timing or the day of the week to get cheaper flights. A Saturday-to-Monday trip is generally cheaper than a Friday-to-Sunday trip. The best day to search for your flight is six Tuesdays before your departure. Make sure that you are booking three weeks out for the best price. You can use Google to confirm that you are purchasing tickets at an economical time. If you are open to traveling on short notice, you can try looking for tickets for departing flights in the next 48 hours. Airlines often discount tickets over the last 48 hours before departure to help fill the plane.

Although pricing trends based on the day of the week are easily discoverable, there are many ways that you can fly cheaper. One approach is to get a connecting flight to your final destination and then skip the final leg of the journey from the connecting flight to the final ticketed destination. This takes advantage of a pricing phenomenon known as "hidden city ticketing." There are companies like Skiplagged that can help you do this. This approach is not without pitfalls. Airline companies hate it, and some will ban or even sue passengers who take advantage of these pricing anomalies.

Another way to take advantage of cheap flights, but this time one that won't get you banned is to use the "map" feature of Google Flights. Suppose that you were searching for a flight from DTW (Detroit International Airport) to Puerto Escondido, Mexico three weeks out. Performing such a search returned some very expensive tickets for Puerto Escondido ($1,122) while also revealing that flights to Aruba ($328), Cancun ($216), or San Jose ($335) were much cheaper for that timeframe while being similar in quality. Having some flexibility on your destination can provide you with much more economical travel.

Saving Money With Google Flights Using the Google Flights map feature can reveal hidden bargains! Compare the price from Detroit to Puerto Escondido (expensive) or to Aruba, San Juan or San José (very reasonable)!

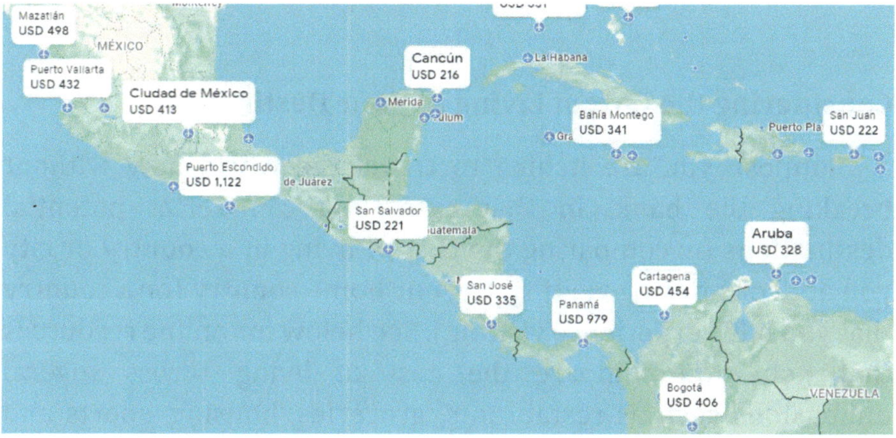

Another great way to get amazing flight deals is to come when others are going. Are you interested in visiting New Orleans, but Mardi Gras isn't your thing? Maybe you have teenage kids for example. Flying in on Ash Wednesday is likely to score you a heavily discounted ticket. The airlines are forced to fly half-empty planes to New Orleans to handle the net outflow of revelers. They might as well discount their tickets to encourage higher occupancy on the way in, and so they do.

If you are firm on destination but flexible on your arrival and departure dates (and with passive income, you should be), you can just click on the "Date Grid" function to find the optimal departure and return dates.

Saving Money with Google Date Grid

Departure < >

Cheapest

Compared with other prices shown

Sun Sep 1	Mon Sep 2	Tue Sep 3	Wed Sep 4	Thu Sep 5	Fri Sep 6	Sat Sep 7	Return
$269	$200	$200	$200	$200	$182	$200	Sun Sep 15
$230	$168	$168	$162	$168	$144	$168	Mon Sep 16
$201	$139	$139	$133	$139	$115	$139	Tue Sep 17
$201	$139	$139	$133	$139	$115	$139	Wed Sep 18
$230	$168	$168	$162	$168	$144	$168	Thu Sep 19
$269	$200	$200	$200	$200	$182	$200	Fri Sep 20
$230	$168	$168	$162	$168	$144	$168	Sat Sep 21

Sep 9 - 18 $138 Round trip

Considering the Cost of Living in Your Destination

Suppose you are itching to travel the world now without breaking the bank. In that case, you can select potential destinations by comparing the cost of living in a country or city you are considering visiting, to your home country (or a country that you have experience visiting). See below for online resources that help you compare the cost of living across several dimensions such as restaurants, groceries, housing, sports and leisure, clothing, and even salaries.

One of the advantages of taking the detailed approach of comparing the cost of living across various dimensions is that it allows you to focus on what is most relevant to you, your tastes, and how long you will be there. Will you be eating in restaurants? Do you have children? Will you stay in a hotel, rent, or even purchase housing?

Online Cost of Living Resources for Travelers on a Budget

- https://www.numbeo.com/cost-of-living/gmaps.jsp for the best interactive map

- https://www.expatistan.com/cost-of-living/index for direct comparisons and a list of the cost of living in 195 major cities and 67 countries.
- https://www.numbeo.com/cost-of-living/compare_countries_result.jsp?country1=Romania&country2=Moldova Just insert your two countries of interest into the URL above

If you are considering working abroad or even becoming a digital nomad, you must consider digital security. A VPN in such situations is a must. You don't want to do anything that will put your own or your client's data in jeopardy.

Passionate Living ($$$)

Do I really need to elaborate here? Once you can afford a lavish lifestyle, the opportunities multiply. This may be a great opportunity to add a concierge or other assistant to make travel and everyday life easier. Living large takes much less imagination when you are truly wealthy!

But Does it Work?

It is fair to take a moment and check in with my personal story to illustrate some of the wins that this approach to life has brought. In 2024, I will have the opportunity to publicly demonstrate my love of Argentine tango in my first showcase. I had the opportunity to become conversational in Spanish in three months through my private lessons. My financial freedom has also given me the time to pursue a love of fashion. I don't have to wear anything "off the rack" unless I choose to. I have had the opportunity to work with fashion designers to produce custom pieces and also self-modify some of my store-bought purchases. My life has become the continuously developing product of an ever-expanding imagination. You can expect more books on the way from this author! I also have the time to freelance as a data scientist from time to time (hey, old habits die hard!).

Protecting Your Fortune

"It requires a great deal of boldness and a great deal of caution to make a great fortune, and when you have got it, it requires ten times as much wit to keep it."

- Mayer Rothschild

As your fortune grows, you will want to ensure that your wealth management plan grows with you. To give you a head start, I will briefly examine taxes, estate planning, succession planning, and wealth management.

Saving Money on Taxes

1031 Exchanges

As your tax bill grows, many options for legal tax avoidance come to the forefront. For real estate investors, one of the greatest tools is the 1031 exchange. This allows you to defer your capital gains so long as you purchase an investment property according to certain rules and restrictions. The bill for a 1031 exchange usually runs between about $600 and $1200, which is trivial considering the tax savings, as we will see below.

To successfully implement a 1031 exchange, you must be aware of a few rules. Most importantly, you must work through a qualified intermediary (QI) throughout the process, who must hold the proceeds from the sale until the purchase of the replacement property is complete. If you wait until after the sale to contact a QI, it is too late.

You will also have to keep track of two important timelines: the 45-day timeline to identify a property and 180 days to close. You can choose three potential replacement properties regardless of fair market value. If the sum of the purchase price of the properties you identify is less than the proceeds from the sale of the property, the difference between the purchase price and proceeds is known as "boot" and is taxable.

The most important question is, of course, how valuable is deferring taxes through a 1031 exchange to wealth-building? The best way to answer this or any similar question is through modeling. Assuming 2x equity multiples and a 20% capital gains tax rate and sales every five years, utilizing a 1031 exchange throughout the process would net you with nearly $1.4 million more in wealth at the end. More importantly, your cash flow will be higher throughout the process with a 1031 because your real estate holdings will be larger without taxes. For example, you would have 50% more cash flow in years 20 to 25.

Notice that Uncle Sam does alright in the end, assuming that the investor fails to continue the 1031 exchange process until death. The 1031 exchange scenario nets the government 81% more in taxes after 25 years for their patience!

Our example here assumes that your final sale at 25 years does not involve a 1031 exchange. If you do continue the 1031 exchange process until death, the contrast in wealth in the 1031 scenario is even more significant. Your heirs will inherit the assets at the stepped-up basis (the value of the assets when you die). This would add $1.8 million to the total of what you would be able to pass on after 25 years. The key lesson of 1031 exchanges is that when it comes to compounding, the timing of taxation is everything.

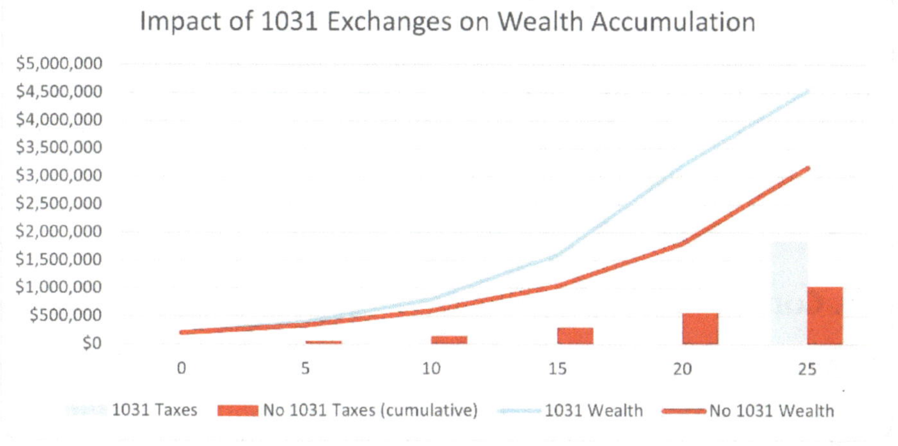

1031 Exchanges Through TIC and DST

You can also use a 1031 exchange to invest in a syndication. The trick is that you must have direct ownership of the property. This can be done through a tenancy in common (TIC) ownership structure. Generally, the minimum investment amount to get into a syndication offering a TIC structure is quite large, often $500,000, due to the additional legal work required to set up the appropriate legal structure.

Another approach to harness the wealth-enhancing power of 1031 exchanges is the Delaware statutory trust (DST). In such a structure, the deeds of one or more properties are held by the DST, thereby providing direct ownership interest. The minimum investment to get into a DST is often significantly smaller than for a syndication through a TIC, often $100,000.

Conservation Easements

If you can no longer manage your need for tax planning through 1031 exchanges and syndications that utilize cost segregation, you can also investigate conservation easements.

Consult the chapter "Passive Investing, a World of Opportunity" for details and caveats. As stated in the disclaimer at the outset, this book is not intended as, nor should it be relied upon to provide tax advice. No book can take into account your unique situation as well as the fact that laws are continually changing.

Tax Consultants

As your needs grow beyond these basic requirements, you may consider hiring a tax consultant. Tax consultants generally work on commission. They generally charge only a fraction of the money that they save you. The catch is that many tax consultants will only take clients above a certain income threshold.

Regardless of whether you currently meet the client threshold, you will definitely want to do your homework to ensure that you are asking the right questions. As with attorneys, the best time to engage a tax consultant is before you need one. After the calendar year is over, there is little that can be done in most cases other than to plan better for the next year. The more you know about taxation, the better you will be positioned to ask the right questions to keep your wealth and your family's wealth safe.

You will want to be aware that as a passive investor, the depreciation you receive is only applicable to passive income such as stock dividends or bond interest coupons. Becoming a real estate professional is the best way to become able to apply passive losses to active income. To become a real estate professional, you will have to spend at least 50% of your professional time on real estate, and you will have to work at least 750 hours per year in real estate. This is not practically possible with a full-time job.

Because real estate professional status is so powerful, it has attracted quite a bit of attention from the IRS. The IRS loves to audit individuals who claim real estate professional status while holding a full-time job. Also, remember that you must show at least 750 hours per year working on real estate. A solid plan for documenting your time will help you sleep well at night.

Diversification

Diversifying across asset classes will help to protect you against catastrophic losses. Deciding which asset classes to invest in is more than just putting some money into real estate, stocks, and operating businesses for example. Consider the significance of your position in the capital stack as well. If you invest in preferred equity positions in six types of real estate, that isn't really diversification. But, if you have a significant portion of your capital invested in first-position debt, then your situation would be much improved.

The bottom of the capital stack pays out first, so when trouble hits, this is the safest place to be. If a wave of foreclosures hits various classes of real estate, at least you can foreclose and become owner of the asset. You may have a headache on your hands to manage the asset, and you may need cash to maintain possession of the asset, but you will be in a much better position than the individual who owned equity in the project and who was faced with a 100% loss.

An Illustration of the Capital Stack

The capital stack of a complex real estate deal is depicted to the right. The exact structure of the capital stack will vary on the basis of deal type. You will want to pay careful attention to where you are in the stack and how likely you are to be paid under various scenarios.

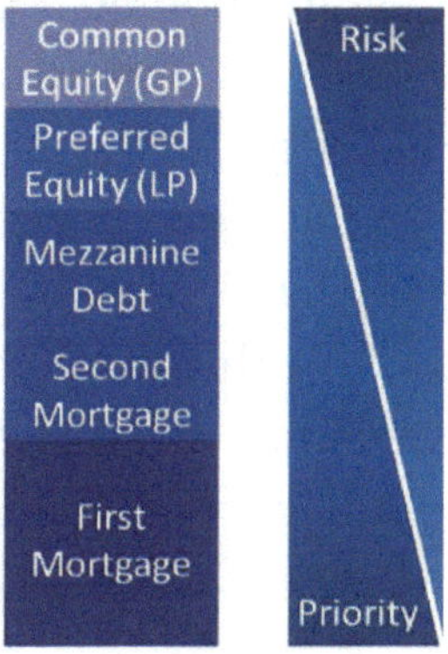

The proportion of your portfolio that should be allocated to private loans should change depending on where we are in the economic and real estate cycle. Having a balance between debt and equity can be valuable from the standpoint of diversification.

The Finest Inheritance

No sooner does a person begin to amass even a small amount of wealth only to be reminded that "you can't take it with you". After a certain point, let's be clear. We really aren't working to satisfy our own desires anymore; we are working mainly with the thought that we are helping the next generation. However, if we are not careful, excess wealth can create entitlement and existential confusion.

Now, imagine leaving your children the finest inheritance. Take a moment to consider what it might look like. Would it consist of silver and gold? Perhaps the family jewels?

Are you ready for my answer? Character. That is the one thing that you can give your children regardless of your level of wealth. And if you give them wealth without passing on your character, you may as well have left them nothing because they aren't likely to know how to hold onto it, even if their intentions are pure. Have you modeled a life of patience and self-restraint? Have you expressed kindness and selflessness? Perhaps the number one personality trait that I have found linked to a positive relationship with money is gratitude. If you are happy with what you have, you already have enough. If you are not happy with what you have, it is unlikely that anything will ever be enough. If you consider love in the same terms, I believe that you will see that the rules are quite the same.

Ensuring that Inheritance Doesn't go to Waste

Most inheritances are spent very quickly. The average time it takes an heir to buy a new car is 19 days. One-third of inheritances are gone within two years[13]. The default is for your hard work to begin to be wasted within days. Now that you know the stakes, it is time to talk about what you can do to turn the odds in your favor.

Your children need to see you living within your means, maintaining spending discipline, and growing your wealth steadily and wisely. You need to teach middle-class values towards money even if you are able to live like money is no object. Never spend money carelessly. Even if you have "money to burn," teach the lesson that $100 is still $100. The money has value, even if you don't need it. There is always something productive that you can do with money, if you feel that you really feel a strong desire to spend. Don't let your kids see you spending like you have "money to burn."

The Importance of Giving

Giving sends a positive tone in more ways than one. Sending the message that money is to be used to help people rather than to gratify immediate desires frames the question of what money represents in a more positive light.

---

[13] "Do People Save or Spend Their Inheritances? Understanding What Happens to Inherited Wealth" *Journal of Family and Economic Issues*, 2012

Building Intergenerational Wealth

You may think that once you have become wealthy that the struggle is over. Alas, if it were only that easy. It turns out that holding onto a fortune may be harder than acquiring it in the first place, at least according to several commentators who have walked the path before.

What one generation earns with great effort, the second-generation values less highly. By the third generation, the character and effort that built the wealth is generally all but lost leaving nothing for the fourth generation. This has been expressed many ways throughout history and across cultures.

"Shirtsleeves to shirtsleeves in three generations"
- Traditional Proverb

"There's nobbut three generations atween a clog and a clog."
- Lancashire Proverb

"Rice paddies to rice paddies in three generations."
- Japanese Proverb

"The father buys, the son builds, the grandchild sells, and his son begs."
- Scottish Proverb

So, you may wonder, what is meant by "shirtsleeves". In the early 1900s, men would often wear jackets in public. It was not uncommon to see a man fishing in a three-piece suit. Women would often fish in a dress. Sometimes even in high heels (check out Joan Wulff, if you don't believe me). Thus, a man dressed simply in "shirtsleeves" (with no jacket) would be seen as having been dressed very casually indeed, presumably indicating poverty.

And what shouldhe modern to make of the historical Lancastrian's rather derisive opinion of clogs? Though available in many exciting colors and styles today, clogs were universally recognized as the dress of the poor one hundred years ago. Their tough wood and leather construction protected laborers from the dangers of agricultural and mining labor and were seen much more as a necessity by those who wore them than the fashion statement they are seen as today.

The foregoing is not meant to discourage ye who desire to build intergenerational wealth, but rather to motivate you - you have your work cut out for you!

Thinking Like the Wealthy

Notice that I said that you need to teach your kids middle-class values when it comes to money (i.e. spending). When it comes to wealth, you need to think like the rich. One way to do that is to pay attention to how family offices, hedge funds, and large pension funds invest. Be aware that institutional investors are beset by fads and misfortune. The idea is to consider carefully the options that lie before you, but never by any means to copy blindly.

Before you start writing out your family values, we can start with a few lessons from my family. From my great grandfather Moilanen on my mother's side, I pass along the following advice to my children, his three rules for life. "Never be too happy or too sad" (keep an even keel). "Be careful what you make a habit of". And finally, "don't let anything get into your system".

From my paternal grandfather George Roberts Senior, I learned the value of hard work and frugality. He was a self-made man who built a fortune during the Great Depression by finding opportunities in the toughest of environments. He owned and operated a family farm and a general store. He also knew how to get down to the point. He would drive more than an hour to see his daughter, but stay only twenty minutes, observing that "Whatever you can't say in twenty minutes isn't worth saying."

From my father, I learned the importance of unflappability in finance. No matter the pressure that financial markets put upon him (and he lived and invested successfully through many a market cycle), he would say "Stocks always come back". Of course, this is not true in every case, but it is a necessary corrective to the hot-blooded emotions that have wrecked many an investing record. Whatever you do, don't panic. From my father, I also learned the importance of discipline, confidence, and thrift. With thrift, you can build capital at any stage of your life, and he did. He read incessantly, reminding me of how Charlie Munger's children would say that their father was "a book with arms". From my mother, a children's librarian, I learned to love reading and the value of education.

Action time! Decide what values your family will pass on to the next generation regarding life and money. Even if you think you have nothing to write, I think you will find that as soon as you begin to recall (and contact your siblings and other living relatives), that you have much more wisdom circulating around you than you imagined. If you happen to be the first financially savvy generation in your family, congratulations - here is your opportunity to make sure that your wisdom is not lost!

From ________ we learned the value of ___________________.

From ________ we learned the value of ___________________.

From ________ we learned the value of ___________________.

From ________ we learned the value of ___________________.

Estate Planning

Although not a pleasant topic, it is never too soon to start thinking about your legacy. Leaving your affairs in good order is more than good financial sense, it is an act of kindness to the next generation. Thoughtful estate planning can avoid a host of troubles and inconveniences for your heirs. You don't want to have to worry about your heirs fighting over your assets and even worse, damaging lifelong relationships.

Proper estate planning requires a lawyer and goes far beyond writing a will. Even the simple act of sitting down with a lawyer and writing a will may be enough to avoid probate in simple situations. There are many additional situations to consider, including the use of trusts, who will take care of the children, and when assets are to be distributed to mitigate "spendthrift" behavior, just to name a few.

You will also want to consider what happens in your LLCs in the event of a partner's death. I always include a clause in all my LLCs that allows partners to transfer their shares to a living trust. There is no reason to let your active investments prevent a clean transfer of assets upon your demise.

From the opposite angle, you may not want to be stuck with a partner's spouse as an active partner upon the event of their death. Succession in such a situation must be spelled out.

Generational Wealth

Families that have been successful in breaking the "three generations" curse have done so through creating a strong family culture. If you are interested in creating generational wealth, the example of the Rockefellers is well worth studying. This family has provided the most successful model of sustained wealth through the transfer of strong family values.

Family Governance

This family, now over 250 strong and in its seventh generation, is still wealthy and meets twice a year. These "Family Forum" meetings are open to all members of the family once they turn 21. Topics discussed in the family forum include family direction, projects, new members, as well as career and other milestones. The family also connects with its past through "homesteads" which refer to the series of estates still owned by the family including Kykuit[14], overlooking the Hudson River and founded by the patriarch of the family.

Rockefeller Family Value #1 Money is a Tool for Charitable Ends

As David Rockefeller Jr. summed it up, "I think the family has tried its best to live those values, 'to whom much is given, much is expected' (Luke 12:8)". John Davison Rockefeller made

---

[14] Kykuit – from Dutch meaning "lookout".

charitable donations from his early paychecks and was donating over 10% by his twenties. The idea that money was not to be sought for its own sake was central to Rockefeller's philosophy, "The man who starts out simply with the idea of getting rich won't succeed; you must have a larger ambition". The idea that wealth is to be used for a greater purpose is exemplified by the following quote "Having been endowed with the gift I possess, I believe it is my duty to make money and still more money, and to use the money I make for the good of my fellow man according to the dictates of my conscience."

Rockefeller Family Value #2 Live Within Your Means

To quote a second-generation Rockefeller, John Davison Jr. "For every right implies a responsibility; every opportunity, an obligation; every possession, a duty." The above inscription memorialized at Rockefeller Center, which he commissioned, clearly summarizes his devotion to the duty of helping others. Though John Davison Sr. certainly enjoyed his wealth, his mansion, Kykuit, is not as opulent as many of his Gilded Age contemporaries. John Davison Sr. also believed in rigorous accounting for purchases. He kept a complete account of all personal purchases throughout his life in a red account book known as "Ledger A" which he kept throughout his life and was stored in a safe deposit box later in his life. (not surprising as he was a bookkeeper early in his career). As observed by Henry Kissinger "I have never known a playboy Rockefeller".

Rockefeller Family Value #3 – Avoid Showy Displays

Not only was his mansion less opulent than those of his contemporaries, John Davison Sr. was also less showy when it came to giving. In philanthropy, he insisted that his name not be emblazoned on every building to which he made a donation. The focus was to be on the good work, not the doer of the deed. Rather than seeing money as a tool for personal aggrandizement, Rockefeller saw it as a byproduct of value creation rather than an end in itself: "I had no ambition to make a fortune. Mere money-making has never been my goal. I saw a marvelous future for our country, and I wanted to participate in the work of making our country great. I had an ambition to build."

Family Offices

For families with assets in the tens of millions, managing the family assets can become onerous. At some point, it becomes necessary to lean on the support of a professional staff to provide various wealth management services. To lessen the overhead, several families may work together with the same group of advisors in an arrangement known as a multi-family office. For families whose net worth is in the $20 million and up range, a virtual family office that offers lighter services may be an appropriate choice for those who don't wish to incur the overhead of a traditional family office.

There is no rush in starting your family office. By the time John Davison Rockefeller founded the first family office in 1882, his net worth in today's dollars was already over $1 billion by some estimates. Not only the first but also the longest-running family office with over 140 years of history.

Infinite Banking

Having great banking relationships is a great way to ensure the liquidity required to continue a successful investing career. "Infinite banking," in which an individual borrows from a life insurance policy to provide liquidity can be a great solution. It is possible to realize returns on the money that you borrow from the cash value of your policy while still retaining the right to earn proceeds on that same money as if it were still in the policy.

Making this work involves ensuring that you have the proper type of policy and that you are operating it efficiently as well. You will want to seek a specialist to ensure that you are operating effectively. Most insurance policies are simply not suited to this approach. If you call an insurance company directly, they may not know about (or, for liability reasons may not be permitted to talk in terms of) "infinite banking".

If you are wondering whether infinite banking works, consider that two of the largest and most visible corporations in the world were started (or purchased) by individuals who borrowed against the value of their whole life insurance policy to obtain their initial capital. I am referring to Ray Kroc and Walt Disney who used the infinite banking concept to get their start.

If you decide that you would like to try infinite banking, you may be faced with the question of what to do with your current policy. Surrendering the policy back to the insurance company is likely to produce a substandard outcome. It is possible to sell your policy on the open market through what is known as a life insurance settlement. It is definitely worthwhile to book a free consultation with an advisor to make sure that you are not leaving money on the table.

Private Banking

Private banking, though less well known, can provide an effective alternative. Banks often extend premium-quality borrowing opportunities to high-net-worth individuals on the basis of a solid balance sheet. Loans may be extended on either a secured or unsecured basis. It is important to be clear on the dangers of such a situation. If you are using equities as collateral, you may find yourself in a world of hurt in the event that you face a margin call or the loan itself is "called" by the bank. The idea behind this book is to use passive investing to have fewer worries, not more.

Wealth Preservation

Whatever your wealth management strategy, realize that once you get to a certain point in your wealth journey, making sure that you hold onto what you have is more important than growing your fortune. You need to think in terms of defense. As long as you have returns high enough to outrun inflation plus what you need to live comfortably, higher returns don't really matter except from the standpoint of taking pride in your investment performance. Quit chasing IRR - the real game is to make sure that you don't end up working for someone again.

Resources for Further Study from George's Award-Winning Podcast "The Foundery – Where Leaders are Forged Daily"

Tax Planning

- Tax-Wise Playbook Part I — Part II
- Saving Millions in Taxes Part I — Part II

Arete: Excellence as a Way of Life

"The true delight is in the finding out rather than the knowing."

- Isaac Asimov

Arete, the goddess of virtue and knowledge, embodied excellence to the ancient Greeks. To her devotees, she was more than a concept, but rather a way of life – the constant striving for excellence, virtue, and fulfillment. It is with this thought that I wish to leave you with gentle reader. You may be headed for the destination of riches, but it is through the journey that you shall find your rewards. Finding freedom from the workaday world need not be the end of activity, but rather an invitation to better quality activity. Activity that is directed solely by your values and your imagination.

Arete - The Greek Embodiment of Excellence

A Life Devoted to Excellence

Meditate for a moment on the role of excellence in your life. Consider how many Greeks were inspired to seek excellence by her image. Maximize your implementation of the suggestions in this book by embodying the spirit of Arete in your personal and financial endeavors.

As you focus on personal growth, consider that trying to become "comfortable with being uncomfortable" leaves you seeking comfort. At best, this is a formula for lukewarm growth. Don't settle for less than you are capable of! Growth is not comfortable. Don't seek to become comfortable in growth. Once you learn to passionately seek the enjoyment and fulfillment that comes with growth and enjoy the process, the byproduct of "pain" becomes inconsequential in comparison to your desire for your chosen goal. Now, that is a recipe for explosive growth!

Remember what it is that is propelling you on your journey. To be impactful, this answer to the question "Why do I do this?" must come from within, but whatever you settled on, it is almost certainly one or more, or a combination of the following: family, faith, and personal development. If you forget what you are truly after, you risk finding yourself on the endless treadmill of conspicuous consumption; the constant search for one more shiny object that will make everything all right. It won't!

I can't promise that you will find a life of fulfillment by chasing experiences, rather than expensive goods, but you will certainly have a better chance. After all, an experience gives you the opportunity to spend time with the people you love, deepening connections and building new memories. Whatever you choose, don't look at your newfound freedom as a destination but rather as a point of departure. An opportunity to build the ideal you that was never far from the surface. Will you be (thinner / more serene and philosophical in your outlook / an artist / closer to your grandkids)? As alluded to in the opening quote for this chapter, you are not likely to be better prepared physically for any adventure than you are at this present moment.

To give you just a brief idea of what I have done since embarking full-time on a lifestyle of entrepreneurship and passive income two and a half years ago, I will list just a few of the things that I have been able to accomplish on the personal and professional level. I lost forty pounds, overcame my lifelong arthritis affliction, and reconnected with my former hobbies, including music and dance. I also found the time to do so many family things that were completely elusive during my tech career, such as doing homework with my children. To have this degree of control over my time and diet would have been inconceivable just a few years ago.

Whatever you choose for yourself, start now! Life is meant to be an adventure – live it to the full! I hope to meet you living your very best life!

Chau,

George

About the Author

George Roberts is a full-time real estate and private equity investor who is as passionate about helping investors master the exciting world of passive investing every bit as much as he is interested in living life's adventure well. He built his passive income streams through investing in a wide range of wealth-building vehicles from real estate to private equity to early-stage companies. Now, he and his family enjoy the fruits of passive income through living a life of connection and adventurous personal growth.

George is the founder of Roberts Capital Enterprises. He owns over 550 units as an active investor and over 800 as an active investor. He is the host of "The Foundery – Where Leaders are Forged Daily," a podcast that explores real estate, entrepreneurship, and finance through dynamic discussion. "The Foundery" has been honored to be named among FeedSpot's Top Apartment Investing Podcasts.

George is also an award-winning data scientist who, in a former life, published heavily cited work in the fields of microbiology, physiology, and genomics. He would love to talk to you about network science and how he earned his Erdős number of 5. George has since repurposed his analytical firepower to make housing economics, macroeconomics, and finance fun and exciting as "The Data Scientist of Real Estate." You can find out more on his YouTube channel, where he brings the pizazz to the discussion of these all-too-often dryly presented topics by presenting them with the animation and liveliness they deserve. Also named Marquis "Who's Who in 2024," George is an award-winning Toastmaster who thoroughly enjoys public speaking. Reach out to have George speak at your next event. You can connect with George at www.robertscapitalenterprises.com.

Connect with the Author

If you found value in this book, George would be happy to connect. Use the scan codes below to continue the conversation!

Data Scientist of Real Estate

The Foundery Podcast

Facebook

Invest with George

CRE Network with George

Instagram

LinkedIn

Twitter (X)

Passionate Investing FB Community

Linktree

Made in United States
Troutdale, OR
11/03/2026

56844899R00096